D1534953

EFFECTIVE MBO

EFFECTIVE MBO

W. J. REDDIN

Associate Professor
Department of Business Administration
University of New Brunswick
Fredericton N.B. Canada

Honorary Visiting Fellow in Behavioural Science
The Management Centre
University of Bradford
Bradford England

Senior Associate
A.I.C. Management Consultants
London England

In collaboration with a team of consultants from
A.I.C. Management Consultants

 Published by Management Publications Limited
for the British Institute of Management

Published by Management Publications Limited
Gillow House 5 Winsley Street London W1

SBN 85118 075 2

First published 1971

Made in Great Britain at the Pitman Press, Bath

Contents

Preface

The aim of this book is to make managers more effective. It enables the manager to set his own objectives. It also gives direct advice to him on how to work with his superior and his subordinates when setting objectives. The book is for the individual manager, not for the MBO specialist. It deals primarily with managerial implementation, not organisational implementation.

The book is designed to be read at home. After reading it a manager should be able to make at least a rough draft of his effectiveness areas and his effectiveness standards. He should then meet with his superior and co-workers to discuss his ideas, and, after discussion, all should agree on them.

For a number of years I have worked with several companies as a change agent. Change agents have been called consultants in behavioural science clothing. The basis of my work was my 3-D Theory of Managerial Effectiveness about which McGraw-Hill published *Managerial Effectiveness* in 1970. The theory deals with effectiveness, management style, the situation and the technology. It could be referred to as a situational theory of management.

I found that a large number of firms used 3-D to implement a programme of Management By Objectives. The use of 3-D in this way wasn't my idea and is certainly not the short way round; but they nevertheless wanted to use it. It became clear to me, as it was to them, that conventional MBO implementation systems did not deal well enough with the human side of things. To put in MBO, or many other systems, successfully the organisation must be unfrozen, the readiness for change must be increased and trust levels and openness and candour must be raised sharply. By and large the 3-D method helped to provide these conditions and this is why it was used.

However, 3-D concerned with managerial effectiveness is not inherently linked with MBO. It occurred to me therefore that I should write a book dealing specifically with MBO and taking as much of 3-D in the process as was needed. As it happens, the two main things needed were the concepts of effectiveness, and that of team implementation. Around these concepts I have written this book as a specific application of the 3-D method, namely to introduce MBO.

Writing this book could be seen as a hiccup in my intellectual career. Why should a behavioural scientist write a book on MBO? I came to MBO quite late. I was a behavioural scientist first and only then a fan of MBO. Some, no doubt, will be reminded of the monologue concerning a press agent talking to Abraham Lincoln, 'Look Abe, we are having a bit of trouble with your biography. Remember, first you were a rail setter, then a lawyer, and not the other way around.' I had to understand MBO, this is the reason the book was written. Without MBO I could not measure managerial effectiveness, let alone organisational effectiveness. MBO has to be the eventual crunch point in organisation change; for why else do we change organisations? It is only to make a system more effective that we change it, and we can understand and measure this by MBO; it is the only way I know, at any rate.

In theory MBO looks like the only way to manage, and perhaps it is. In practice it often becomes a bureaucratic overlay or a powerful scheme of seduction – 'management wanted autocracy, but they couldn't sell it, so they disguised it as MBO and fooled all of us for about eighteen months.' Alert managers have realised that current MBO theory and practice are far apart. This book tries to explain and close the gap. While MBO is popular it has also more clear failures than successes. Some consulting firms spend more time taking MBO out than putting it in.

The Effective MBO explained in this book is most often used for second generation MBO implementations. These situations occur when an attempt to implement MBO runs into some road blocks which are not fully overcome.

This book specifically does not present a new MBO. I have no idea what one would be. Through its two contributions of effectiveness and team implementation, however, it can strengthen existing methods. Nothing in this book is in serious disagreement with Odiorne's or Humble's works on the subject. Only the emphasis is different. We now have the technical knowledge to design effective organisations around the outputs of individual managerial positions. We also now have the social knowledge to be able to allow individual managers to do their best in working towards these outputs so let's use them.

The book, I hope, will be seen as making two main contributions. One is the logical development of the concept of effectiveness by which to describe managerial positions. This takes up the first two thirds of the book. The second is the formal implementation techniques based heavily on the team. This takes up the last third of the book.

I hope, of course, that this book will be seen as an original contribution. If I had not hoped that, I would never have written it. This book both summarises what is now known about **MBO** and also extends what is known. I have taken several long walks while thinking through two ideas in this book: the concepts of alignment of effectiveness areas and that of common effectiveness areas. All the other MBO books I have read glossed over them so I had to work them out myself. While Chapters Four and Seven may not seem a startling contribution to those unfamiliar with MBO, I hope that some will see what importance the ideas in these chapters can have in implementing **MBO** effectively.

In case anyone should want to know, I am fully 'on MBO'. My five-year and one-year objectives are established, and detailed plans made for all of them on **ORS** forms (Chapter 11). My effectiveness areas are: innovation, propagation and exploitation. The first two are common to any academic; the third reflects my practical, some say commercial, bent. I review my success or failure in January each year. I have in front of me now my 'activity schedule' which outlines which of my activities (page 127) I wish to complete during these first few months of 1971. Using MBO personally has helped me enormously in achieving managerial effectiveness and job satisfaction: I hope it does the same for the readers of this book.

I have tried to keep the book relatively free of behavioural science jargon; which will surprise many of my friends. The implementation method however is rich with behavioural science practice. The book is behavioural science in practice.

Drafts of this book were tested in the United States, Canada, United Kingdom, Australia, Ireland, and Argentina. Companies ranging in size from 100 to 5,000 employees have implemented these methods. Well over 80,000 managers have been exposed to and have critically evaluated the 3-D Theory of Managerial Effectiveness, on which the concept of effectiveness is based.

W. J. REDDIN
Bradford
Yorkshire

Acknowledgements

I want to acknowledge the important contributions to the basic ideas of this book obtained from the writings of Peter Drucker, George Odiorne, John Humble, and Douglas McGregor.

Several members of Associated Industrial Consultants assisted in many ways. Harry Jamieson, of that Company, had useful things to contribute on every chapter and assisted me greatly in developing the concepts of effectiveness standards and common effectiveness areas.

I am also indebted to those who provided opportunities to test the application of the book, Reg Tweeddale, Derek Oland, Dick Toner, Bill Morrow and Jack Estey.

Carl West-Mead and Allen Ainsworth of John Player & Sons visited me at Monk Fryston Hall in Yorkshire and criticised an early draft in no uncertain terms. It would not have been so bad, but they were drinking my scotch at the time. Because of them Chapter Twelve was written. I took their advice on certain other matters, however, and must specifically disclaim responsibility for any errors they may have caused me to introduce into the book. Alert members will no doubt spot such contributions.

My special thanks go to Bob Busvine, Patrick Kehoe, Denis Ryan, and Charles Tennant, for their numerous detailed suggestions concerning the final draft manuscript. Their comments were directly helpful in making this a more useful book for managers.

I am grateful to Jorge Chapiro and Bernard Hippsley who provided helpful ideas on various parts of the book and to Jean Hossack who typed all my drafts with her customary dedication and care.

Denis Ryan made a distinct contribution while walking with me through Deer Park at Richmond, when he said, 'Concentrate on clarity, not richness'. A small sign to that effect is in front of me now. I hope it has had some effect.

W.J.R.

DEDICATION

To the three men who have most influenced MBO – Peter Drucker, John Humble and George Odiorne.

part one

THE MEANING OF MBO

1 What is Managerial Effectiveness?

Some managers le. the in-basket define the nature of their contribution and the clock its limit.

In every firm some managers could be retired at full salary and profits would go up.

Duties constrain managers, objectives liberate them.

Many managers believe that if they are not behind their desk they are not working.

Most executives could redesign their work, set clear objectives, contribute far more, and work an hour or less a day.

The MBO system described in this book has many similarities to and differences from other systems. Its single most important difference is the emphasis and meaning it gives to managerial effectiveness.

There is only one realistic and unambiguous definition of managerial effectiveness: effectiveness is the *extent to which a manager achieves the output requirements of his position*. The concept of managerial effectiveness is the central issue in management. It is the manager's job to be effective. It is his only job.

1.1 Three kinds of effectiveness

The idea of managerial effectiveness can be clearly understood when managers learn to distinguish sharply between:

> Managerial effectiveness
> Apparent effectiveness
> Personal effectiveness

3

Managerial effectiveness, apparent effectiveness and personal effectiveness are quite different from each other.

1.1.1 *Managerial effectiveness*

Managerial effectiveness is not an aspect of personality. It is not something a manager has. To see it this way is nothing more or less than a return to the now discarded trait theory of leadership, which suggested that more effective leaders had special qualities not possessed by less effective leaders. Effectiveness is best seen as something a manager produces from a situation by managing it appropriately. It represents output, not input. The manager must think in terms of performance, not personality. It is not so much what a manager does, but what he achieves. As an extreme example:

> A manager's true worth to his company may sometimes be measured by the amount of time he could remain dead in his office without anyone noticing it. The longer the time, the more likely it is that he makes long run policy decisions rather than short run administrative decisions. The key decisions in a company are long-run and may refer to market entry, new product introduction, new plant location, or key man appointments. The person making these should not get involved, as can happen, with short-run issues. If he does, he has not decided on the output measures of his job or has not the skill or opportunity to create conditions where only policy issues reach him.

Once a manager has decided he wants to become effective he should initially focus on how he can contribute more or contribute more effectively than he is now doing. Some managers have narrow views of their jobs. What they do they may do well, but what they leave undone is enormous. Some managers let the in-basket define the nature of their potential contribution and the clock its limit. One manager might view his contribution as simply that of managing a going concern and keeping it on an even keel, while another might see the

same job as having large components of subordinate development and creative problem solving in it. Still another might
see his position primarily as a lynch pin connecting with other
parts of the firm, and thus might take a wider view of his
responsibility.

Specialists seldom focus on contributions. They often see
themselves simply as a knowledge bank: 'I am not paid for
what I do but for what I know.' This view can and does
insulate the specialist from the firm, the professor from the
student, and the university from society.

Managerial effectiveness can seldom be obtained by achieving a single objective, no matter how broadly it is written.
Profit, for instance, may be obtained at the risk of losing
customers or by sacrificing human resources. Any manager
who sees his effectiveness criteria in simple black-and-white
terms may perform well in the short run but may not in the
long run. Effectiveness is multidimensional.

Before a manager can operate with full effectiveness he must:

> Understand the overall contribution his unit should
> make, which means knowing what his superior is re-
> sponsible for.

> Understand his role in his unit, which means knowing
> what he is responsible for achieving and knowing what
> his superior thinks is a good job.

> Establish specific objectives which he intends to achieve
> in a determined time period.

> Have the help of his superior in overcoming obstacles
> which may prevent the attainment of these objectives.
> These obstacles may lie in the organisation, the job, the
> superior or the manager himself.

> Have a willingness to work to achieve his objectives
> which may mean preparedness to change his behaviour.

> Receive concrete periodic feedback on his progress
> towards his objectives.

> Receive help and guidance as he needs it.

> Be held responsible for his actions over the longer term.

If any of these are missing, full effectiveness is unlikely to occur.

A well designed organisation usually ensures that managerial effectiveness, and only managerial effectiveness, leads to personal rewards. While organisations do vary in the extent, speed, and adequacy of rewards for effectiveness there can be little doubt that, in the long run, the effective manager is the rewarded one. The rewards are usually concrete in terms of salary, level of position, and advancement rate. Together with these, and more important to some, are fulfilled ambitions, assured security, self actualisation, personal satisfaction or happiness, or simply survival.

1.1.2 *Apparent effectiveness*

It is difficult, if not impossible, to judge managerial effectiveness by observation of behaviour alone. The behaviour must be evaluated in terms of whether or not it is appropriate to the output requirements of the job. For example, these qualities, important in some jobs, may in others be irrelevant to effectiveness:

> Usually on time
> Answers promptly
> Makes quick decisions
> Good at public relations
> Good writer

These usually give an air of apparent effectiveness in no matter what context they appear. But apparent effectiveness may or may not lead to managerial effectiveness.

> Charles Smith was an independent consultant in Australia, with four employees. He was first in and last out each day. He virtually ran everything and ran everywhere. In a business which usually makes low demands for immediate decisions, he always made them on the spot. 'Do it now' was his catch phrase. Very intelligent, active, optimistic, and aggressive, his job input was

enormous. His staff turnover, however, in one year was 100 per cent and he sometimes signed contracts which he had no possibility of meeting. If his business fails, the casual observer may well say, 'It wasn't because of Charlie,' thus showing the confusion over the important differences between apparent effectiveness and managerial effectiveness.

Conventional job descriptions often lead to an emphasis on what could be called 'managerial efficiency', the ratio of output to input. The problem with this is that even if both input and output are low, efficiency could still be 100 per cent. In fact, a manager or department could easily be 100 per cent efficient and 0 per cent effective. The efficient manager is easily identified. He prefers to:

Do things right	*rather than*	Do right things
Solve problems	*rather than*	Produce creative alternatives
Safeguard resources	*rather than*	Optimise resource utilisation
Discharge duties	*rather than*	Obtain results

Conventional job descriptions lead to the kind of thinking on the left side; job effectiveness descriptions lead to that shown on the right.

Conventional job descriptions and, for that matter, management audits, usually focus on the internal efficiency of an organisational system rather than its external effectiveness or its outputs. It would be a simple matter to increase internal efficiency sharply and to decrease external effectiveness just as sharply. Paper work is usually quite unrelated to effectiveness.

1.1.3 *Personal effectiveness*

Poorly defined job outputs can also lead to what might be called 'personal effectiveness', that is the satisfying of personal objectives rather than the objectives of the organisation. This is particularly likely to occur with ambitious men in an organisation which has only a few clearly defined management output measures. Meetings with these men are riddled with hidden agendas which operate below the surface and lead to poor decision making.

In a three day meeting to set corporate objectives for a Toronto consumer goods firm one of the four vice presidents present initiated a series of proposals for reorganisation and argued for them with great force. While all had some merit, it became clear as he described them that most would not lead to greatly improved team effectiveness. Other team members saw quickly that all these proposals were aimed, to some extent unconsciously, at improving the vice president's power and prestige. This issue was confronted for several hours and the team members, many of whom had previously had intentions similar to those of the vice president, finally decided to turn their attention away from improving their personal effectiveness towards improving their managerial effectiveness and, therefore, their total team effectiveness. The top management structure was modified, but in keeping with market, consumer, competitive, and organisational needs, not personal needs.

1.2 Is your job described in terms of managerial effectiveness?

The work a manager is expected to accomplish, or the behaviour or outputs expected of him, is usually described in one of two ways:

Conventional job description — focus on input behaviour of position

Job effectiveness description – focus on output of position

The use of job effectiveness descriptions is likely to improve managerial effectiveness: the use of the other type is likely to inhibit it.

8

1.2.1 *Conventional job descriptions emphasise inputs*

The source of much of the problem surrounding effectiveness is found in the way job descriptions are written. Lengthy job descriptions, or crash programmes to write them or up-date them, usually have little actual usefulness. As Parkinson has pointed out, the last act of a dying organisation is to issue a revised and greatly enlarged rule book. This observation may hold as well for crash programmes to write job descriptions.

Many, if not most, managerial jobs are defined in terms of their input and behaviour requirements by such phrases as:

> 'He administers'
> 'He maintains'
> 'He organises'
> 'He plans'
> 'He schedules'

Naturally enough, managers never refer to job descriptions like these. Once made they are not very useful as an operating guide. They are often proposed initially by those who want to use a seemingly scientific technique to justify a widespread change in salary differentials or a change in the organisation structure. They are often a negative influence as they focus on input and behaviour, the less important end of the manager's job. Some managers focus on their job input by saying; 'I manage 1,200 people' rather than by speaking in terms of output; 'I am responsible for expanding at 6 to 10 per cent a year with product A and B with my existing resources.' One is the conventional job description approach; the other is the job effectiveness description approach.

As Dale McConkey has said:

> '. . . those companies which point with pride to fat job descriptions which state in lofty terms that a vice president of purchasing, for example, "is responsible for formulating, establishing, and administering an effective purchasing programme". A prodigious amount of paper and effort could be saved if these companies merely said that the vice president of purchasing "purchases" – most of them

9

would lose little by this abbreviated version because many of their descriptions say little more in any case. They may state the particular functional area of activity for which a manager is responsible, but certainly they do not enumerate the results for which the manager is accountable within that area of activity, and they do not mention the time element during which the results must be achieved. Moreover, the same job description may remain on the books for several years, even though the enterprise's overall targets may have changed several times during those years.'

Some MBO schemes are in fact based on input descriptions. Here one finds such objectives as 'Answer letters within two days' or 'Have all reports in on time'. All of these sound like important objectives, and all are measurable. The problem is that, while they may be important, all are really inputs and, for most positions, have nothing to do with why the position was created.

Some organisations have a predominance of job descriptions which focus on a manager's position in the organisation.

'He reports to'
'He authorises'
'He co-ordinates'
'He delegates'
'He approves'

This kind of job description can be important to the services in wartime, when changes in command can take place in seconds, but focusing as they do on structure they spring from and reinforce the bureaucratic style. Many senior officers who participate in effectiveness training are surprised to see evidence mount up that they are bureaucrats and that they work essentially from a position description framework with little attention to output.

One such officer, a general, was the director of a large Canadian army command in peacetime. He found that in situational training exercises he first looked for rules to guide him and then for approval of his action by his superior. He frequently used 'I submit' as a verbal prelude to an argument. There was little doubt that this style was appropriate for his peacetime job. He had no real output measures to guide him. He was subject to tight control from Ottawa. His job, in fact, was equivalent to that of the principal of a technical college, maintaining a going concern, which processed raw recruits at one end, changing them to a trained force, and then improved this level of training and readiness until their retirement at the age of forty-five or fifty.

Position descriptions without objective standards of output associated with them can lead to the maintenance of managers in a business organisation who are not contributing to the organisation in any useful way.

1.2.2 *Job effectiveness descriptions emphasise outputs*
The job effectiveness description is quite another matter. Its purpose is to help a manager become effective. It does this by almost exclusively dealing with the position in output terms. It contains a list of the effectiveness areas of the position. These are the general output requirements of the manager's position and might, for instance, include such words as 'sales' or 'costs'. Together with each of the effectiveness areas are one or more effectiveness standards which are specific output requirements. From 'sales' as the effectiveness areas, 'sales of product A in Area B' might be derived as the effectiveness standard. Associated with each effectiveness standard the manager develops a specific objective, usually annually, and he measures his degree of attainment of the objective by the established measurement method, also contained in the job effectiveness descriptions. For most managers all of this can be contained on one side of one piece of paper. The only additional content of the job effectiveness descriptions are specific statements of the authority vested in the position. These statements may refer to authority to enlarge or decrease staff, use overtime, change the product

or service, rearrange work flow or modification of a production programme. In constructing these job effectiveness descriptions great care is taken to ensure that the authority is sufficient for the specified effectiveness standards and the objectives derived from them. Either the authority is found or made sufficient or the effectiveness areas and effectiveness standards are passed upward.

Job effectiveness descriptions are prepared for each managerial position and also for each unit which would include a manager and all of his subordinates. Managerial objectives are thus formally linked to team objectives.

The main purpose of this book is to teach in a hopefully interesting way how to develop job effectiveness descriptions, how to obtain commitment to them, and how to breathe life in them so a true Effective MBO is produced.

Before moving into the methods by which a manager can best see his job in output terms it will be useful to clarify what management by objectives really means. Naturally it can mean different things in different companies. The next chapter explains the elements common to most MBO systems and the non common or essentially optional elements.

New concepts introduced – Chapter 1

At the end of each chapter the key concepts introduced in it are defined in alphabetical order. The 'Effective MBO Dictionary' at the end of the book lists all the concepts.

APPARENT EFFECTIVENESS:
> The extent to which a manager gives the appearance of being effective.

JOB EFFECTIVENESS DESCRIPTION (JED):
> A written statement specifying the effectiveness areas, effectiveness standards and authority of a particular managerial position.

CONVENTIONAL JOB DESCRIPTION:

A written statement emphasising the input requirements of a particular managerial position.

MANAGERIAL EFFECTIVENESS (E):

The extent to which a manager achieves the output requirements of his position.

PERSONAL EFFECTIVENESS:

The extent to which a manager achieves his own private objectives.

2 MBO Today

MBO in the United States is centred on motivating the individual while MBO in Britain is centred on corporate planning. Each could learn from the other.

Management by objectives is a powerful management tool and may even be considered a method of managing. Its abbreviation, 'MBO', is known to most managers and will continue to be.

The ideas behind MBO were popularised by Peter Drucker in the early 1950s. The name most associated with MBO currently in the United States is George Odiorne; in the United Kingdom it is John Humble. There are now about twenty books on MBO. The best known of the authors are Odiorne, Batten, Drucker, Humble, Mahler, Miller, Wickstrom and Valentine.

Versions of MBO go under a variety of names. The most widely used are:

> Management by results
> Goals management

Whatever it is called, MBO is now in use around the world and in many major companies in the United Kingdom and the United States, for instance:

United Kingdom	United States
Barclays Bank	Air Force Logistics Command
British Leyland Motor Corporation	Du Pont
Colt International	General Electric
Ministry of Defence	General Foods
John Player and Sons	General Motors
Scottish Gas Board	Radio Corporation of America
Smiths Industries	Socony Mobil Oil
South Western Electricity Board	Standard Oil

There must be something to it.

What is MBO? What is common to all MBO systems? What are the major differences among them? This chapter will answer these questions.

2.1 Points of view

MBO, like anything else, may be looked at from many different points of view. Looking solely at its head, one thinks of corporate planning or strategy. Looking solely at its tail one thinks of appraisal. It is entirely appropriate that MBO should mean different things to different companies. If a company is good at planning but poor at operating its use and view of MBO will be somewhat different from that of a company in the opposite position.

Humble's definition of MBO shows clearly the importance he places on corporate planning (emphasis added): 'A dynamic system which integrates *the company's need to achieve its goals* for profit and growth, with the manager's need to contribute and develop himself. It is a demanding and rewarding style of managing a business', while Odiorne's definition stresses the manager and his superior rather more (emphasis added): '*the superior and the subordinate managers of an organisation jointly* define its common goals, define each individual's major areas of responsibility in terms of the results expected of him and use these measures as guides for operating the unit and assessing the contribution of each of its members.'

Some theorists go so far as to suggest that MBO is primarily a contract between a superior and his subordinates. Others see its essence as a downward extension of corporate planning. These kinds of differences need to be worked out prior to the decision to implement – not halfway through the programme.

The definition of MBO used in this book is:

The establishment of effectiveness areas and effectiveness standards for managerial positions

and the periodic conversions of these into measurable time bounded objectives linked vertically
and horizontally and with future planning.

Effective MBO then is seen as a method of associating
objectives with positions and linking these objectives together
and with the corporate plan. The method of implementation
used is not part of the definition.

Clearly while all three definitions are different there are
many common elements.

2.2 Common elements in MBO systems

The major common elements in MBO systems are:

> Objectives established for positions
> Use of joint objective setting
> Linking of objectives
> Emphasis on measurement and control
> Establishment of a review and re-cycle system
> High involvement of superior
> High staff support in early stages

That is, clear objectives are set for managerial positions,
most often jointly by superior and subordinate; attempts are
made to link objectives with those of other relevant positions;
a great emphasis is put on quantification, measurement and
control and a regular review is made, usually bi-annually.
The superior initiates a great deal, except in the early stages,
when a high degree of staff support is common.

2.2.1 *Objectives established for positions*
MBO is based squarely on setting objectives for managerial
positions. These at higher levels may be called 'goals', 'targets',
or 'aims', but the basic idea is the same – to decide what the
manager in the position is required to achieve. Most but not
all MBO systems require numerical and time bounded

statements of objectives. A few allow 'subjective' statements for staff positions. For any particular position there may be one or over ten objectives. Most systems suggest from four to eight objectives.

2.2.2 Use of joint objective setting

Most MBO systems employ some kind of joint objective setting. Both superior and subordinate participate in the objective-setting process. There still is much confusion within particular systems and among them as to just what is meant by 'participation'. In most the superior does the preliminary work; in some a consultant does almost all of it. As a minimum, the subordinate's participation is simply his presence at a meeting and a right to be heard. At its maximum it means that the subordinate initiates job redesign proposals and has a strong upward influence.

2.2.3 Linking of objectives

While not always emphasised in the basic texts some form of linking of objectives is a part of all MBO systems. This means, in its simplest form, that if marketing has an objective of selling 100,000 units, production has an objective of producing 100,000 units. Such linking as this is virtually automatic, and if it does not occur, then very loud feedback is usually obtained. More sophisticated linking can take place among staff and line, not so much over quantity, but in the timing of parts of plans which must fit together.

2.2.4 Emphasis on measurement and control

While few systems go as far as to say, 'If you can't measure it, forget it', all do emphasise the necessity of being able to measure results and of being able to control them. If an objective cannot be measured its attainment cannot be known. If an objective cannot be subject to control, it is simply a prediction and not an objective. MBO implementations are often held up because of poor measurement and control systems.

2.2.5 *Establishment of a review and re-cycle system*

All MBO systems have some form of review of progress toward objectives, some action is taken and then new objectives are set for the next period. The typical cycle goes something like:

> Objectives Set for Year 1
> First Progress Check
> Second Progress Check
> Objectives Set for Year 2

This review is always between the superior and the subordinate.

2.2.6 *High involvement of superior*

Most MBO systems involve the superior more than the subordinate. In some the superior sets the objectives, 'sells' them, measures them, and evaluates progress. This process is sometimes so widespread that it should be called 'control by objectives' not 'management by objectives'.

2.2.7 *High staff support in early stages*

Few organisations are so well designed or have managers so well trained that MBO can be put in without trained staff support. The do-it-yourself film kits are of value, but they do not and could not put in an MBO system by themselves. At most they can only provide a dry run.

2.3 Other elements in MBO systems

In theory all MBO programmes are essentially as just described. In actual practice, however, many major differences are apparent. In the United Kingdom MBO has a very great emphasis on what is called 'corporate planning' or 'strategy' and on the internal MBO adviser. A programme to introduce it there may take twelve months before it gets out of the board room. In the United States, while corporate planning is often the focus of MBO, individual motivation is seen as a prime condition and appraisal is still an important focus of attention. Much more emphasis is spent on aspects of human needs and participative techniques. In Canada a lead has been taken in MBO by the Federal Government. This as in other such administrative settings elsewhere, has tended to emphasise appraisal rather than strategy or motivation. The programme tends to be introduced by the personnel department as a substitute for standard merit rating forms. However, the underlying approach to all three methods is the same. It includes the clarification of managerial position outputs and then the derivation of specific measurable objectives. How the objectives are derived, and what overall emphasis is put on individual commitment or appraisal are, however, major differences to be considered.

So, while having many similarities, MBO systems do vary from one another in the emphasis they give to:

Corporate planning
Manager planning
Appraisal link
Rewards link
Position analysis made
Motivation element
Participation element
Emphasis on future

2.3.1 *Corporate planning*

Is MBO an expression of the five year plan at manager level or is it a contract between two individuals or is it both? Should MBO start anywhere but at the top? Is MBO a way of the executive committee making sure their needs are met, or a way of insuring a manager's needs are met? If the needs conflict, which takes precedence? Can an individual really participate in MBO if the company also wants to develop a highly integrated plan?

These kinds of questions reflect a central difference among MBO systems. While things are not quite so black and white, the essential difference remains one of the degree of emphasis on corporate planning or the individual. Clearly both are important, but in practice one or the other is given emphasis.

2.3.2 *Manager planning*

MBO systems differ in the extent to which a manager is expected to make a plan to achieve the objective agreed. Effective MBO stresses manager planning a great deal. An objective without a plan is either a dream or simply a prediction specifying what would happen anyway with much effort. Stating an objective can be easy, making a plan to ensure it is met is quite another thing.

The plan the manager creates is his business, not that of his superior. The objective is agreed with his superior, the plan is designed and implemented by the manager himself. What a manager is to achieve needs agreement with his superior, how he plans to do it is his business.

The absence of formal manager planning could well be a central problem in many MBO approaches. Objectives tend to be rather glorious but it is logistics which deliver them.

General Ridgeway said: 'What throws you in combat is rarely the fact that your tactical scheme was wrong – though, of course, history is replete with examples of faulty tactical planning – but that you failed to think through the hard cold fact of logistics. You failed to ask yourself, "how am I going to get Force A from X to Y and how am I going to supply and sustain it once it gets there?" There is always a great temptation to think only of the objective to be attained, to ignore the basic planning in the hope that in some way the Lord will provide.'

2.3.3 *Appraisal link*

No matter how the particular form of MBO is designed, if it is implemented by the personnel department it becomes an appraisal scheme.

A survey of one firm by Tosi and Carroll produced this view in response to the questions: 'What are the purposes of the programme as you see them and what is the rationale for this approach?'

Philosophy and Rationale of the Objectives Approach

			%
1	To link evaluation to performance .	17	35·4
2	Aid manager in planning . . .	12	25·0
3	Motivate managers. . . .	11	22·9
4	To increase boss/subordinate interaction and feedback	11	22·9
5	Development of management potential	8	16·6
6	Link company objectives to department objectives	8	16·6
7	Managers know what their job is .	6	12·5
8	Give management information about what's going on at lower levels . .	4	8·3
9	Management club to pressure performance	3	6·25
10	No mention	7	14·5

Notice that over 35 per cent saw it as an appraisal scheme and that this was chosen more times than any other description. While MBO is useful for appraisal it can come to be seen as a 'do-it-yourself hangman's kit'. The strength of MBO is in motivation, in planning and in integrating the sub-parts of the firm. If the major emphasis is on appraisal or on getting more by squeezing harder then the whole point of MBO is lost.

2.3.4 *Rewards link*

MBO systems differ sharply in the emphasis they give to the link between performance and rewards such as salary, promotion or greater responsibility. Most suggest that the discussion of performance should be separated from the salary review. Some actually go so far as to suggest that what goes on between a superior and a subordinate concerning the degree of attainment of an objective should not be considered during salary review. One could ask why then should a manager exert more effort. An attempt to make a one-year link between objectives and rewards is naïve, but no link at all is criminal. Such links, even long term ones, should not be seriously attempted until MBO has been working well for a few years.

2.3.5. *Position analysis made*

Some MBO programmes start with what amounts to a complete description of the job. About eight to twelve hours are spent with each manager in working out just what his job is. The following is an example:

> This analysis is not a job description of the usual sort. It specifies not only the main areas of responsibility of the job-holder, but also the actual results to be achieved and targets to be hit, and the means by which progress can be measured and monitored. It contains specific suggestions for improvements wherever these appear to be possible. We have found that initially most managers need a great deal of help in thinking through their jobs in this new way, and in fact usually require four or five two-hour sessions spread over several weeks to allow for careful thought and analysis between sessions, before their minds are adjusted to thinking in terms of specific results and controls.

Other systems ignore this or give it very little emphasis. The assumption is, and it may be a good one, that before embarking on an MBO programme, a firm should have a clear idea of the function of each position.

Some problems can arise with lengthy position analysis programmes. The most important problem is that part of the analysis is usually pure input, and talking about it may teach managers the wrong thing.

There is the valid point that to spend time on getting complete agreement on 'main purpose of the job', its 'structural position in the organisation', its 'scope', its 'authority' and so forth, may only hinder the determining of the effectiveness areas.

However, once such a position description is complete, no one wants to do it again as it takes so much time. Effectiveness areas should come first, around which job effectiveness descriptions can then be written.

2.3.6 *Motivation element*

If properly introduced MBO has a high motivational content, especially if objectives are mutually set with superiors, if the superior is seen more as a coach and less as a judge, and if those who consistently perform well are ultimately rewarded. Some top managers mistakenly see MBO primarily as a control and appraisal tool. It certainly is both of these, but this is not the central idea.

MBO can demotivate if each manager is simply handed his objectives and told to 'get on with it'. This method is usually associated with an emphasis on control procedures. Methods like this have worked, of course, but better methods exist. The immediate result may be more activity; the long term result, however, is that managers have no sense of autonomy. They tend to 'play it safe' and so they prefer objectives that are easy to meet rather than those that represent an optimistic view of what is possible.

2.3.7 *Participation element*

MBO cannot be clearly related to participative management as 'participative management' has such a wide range of meanings. At one extreme, 'What I mean by participative management is that our employees will get more involved with their own work, and I am going to introduce it here no matter how hard I must push for it.' This may sound like a caricature but it is a virtually verbatim quote from a Canadian federal government deputy minister.

At the other extreme, 'Participative management to have any meaning, must allow workers to redesign their jobs, change salary differentials in their department, and propose modifications in the responsibilities of their superior. Without all this participation is a fiction.' Somewhere between these extremes most of us stand. The point is that it is unwise to use the word *participation* unless a clear agreement exists as to what the user means by the term.

MBO may or may not be related to increasing or decreasing degrees of delegation. In practice MBO often leads to increased delegation, but it does not have to do so. MBO may well lead to the discovery that a subordinate is held responsible for things for which he has not, and could not be given, authority. In this case the superior, not the subordinate, could end up with a larger job than he started with. This would be delegation upward, or centralisation.

2.3.8 *Emphasis on future*

Like Scrooge's ghosts, effectiveness has its past, its present, and its future. MBO can be designed around any one or any combination of these three time orientations. The past emphasises 'appraisal', the present emphasises coaching, while the future emphasises outputs in the true sense.

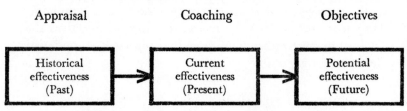

| Appraisal | Coaching | Objectives |

Figure 1   From appraisal to objective setting

(*MBO gets managers to look forward rather than backward*)

Elements of appraisal and coaching are still part of MBO but the better emphasis is on learning from the past and harnessing the resources of the present to become effective in the future.

2.4 Forms of MBO

So obviously MBO can exist in several forms. It has common elements in all forms and elements which may or may not be present in individual forms.

Common elements	*Optional elements*
Objective for positions	Corporate planning
Joint objective setting	Manager planning
Linking of objectives	Appraisal link
Measurement and control	Rewards link
Review and re-cycle	Position analysis
High involvement of superior	Motivation element
High staff support	Participation element
	Emphasis on future

The form MBO takes in the organisation depends on the type of system used, which function has responsibility for it, and what happens in the first year.

The system described in this book shares the common elements. Of the optional elements it emphasises the first two and the last four listed. Its central theme, however, is the concept of effectiveness.

New concept introduced – Chapter 2

MANAGEMENT BY OBJECTIVES (MBO):

> The establishment of effectiveness areas and effectiveness standards for managerial positions and the periodic conversion of these into measurable time-bounded objectives linked vertically and horizontally and with future planning.

part two

EFFECTIVENESS AREAS

3 Effectiveness Areas and Standards

It is impossible to appraise a manager without knowing the output requirements of his position.

The concept of effectiveness is the only sound basis of MBO.

Effective MBO puts great emphasis on the four concepts of managerial effectiveness, effectiveness areas, effectiveness standards and objectives. This chapter shows how they are related. Many other MBO systems use one or more similar ideas but not usually with the same emphasis.

3.1 Four concepts

Managerial effectiveness
> The extent to which a manager achieves the output requirements of his position.

Effectiveness areas
> General output requirements of a managerial position.

Effectiveness standards
> Specific output requirements and measurement criteria of a managerial position.

Objectives
> Effectiveness standards which are as specific, as time-bounded, and as measurable as possible.

While the idea of 'objectives' is central in MBO, the other three ideas, 'managerial effectiveness', 'effectiveness areas', and 'effectiveness standards' are the foundation of any objectives that are set. Only with an understanding of these foundations will the objectives be sound.

3.1.1 *Managerial effectiveness*

A sound implementation of MBO must be preceded by the acceptance of managerial effectiveness as the central value or philosophy in management. Unless this is given primary importance, MBO will be no more than a highly sophisticated managerial level work study. A small, or even a large, firm can have values built in which counter the idea of managerial effectiveness. Such values may seriously interfere with or completely prevent the implementation of MBO.

3.1.2 *Effectiveness areas*

The second idea, effectiveness areas, is based on the view that all managerial positions are best seen in terms of the outputs associated with them. Surprisingly few managers see their positions this way.

A complete set of effectiveness areas for the position of sales manager could be:

> Sales policies
> Sales levels
> Sales costs
> Line profitability

While for a production manager they could be:

> Production level
> Delivery times
> Cost levels
> Quality level
> Inventory control
> Machine utilisation

Effectiveness areas spring primarily from the strategy of the firm as made operational by the organisation structure. To a lesser but still significant extent they depend on top management's views on the best locus for decision making.

3.1.3 *Effectiveness standards*

Effectiveness standards are subdivisions of effectiveness areas which incorporate measurement criteria explicitly or implicitly. An effectiveness area of 'sales' might be conveniently broken down into one or more of these sets of effectiveness standards:

> Existing products—existing markets
> Existing products—new markets
> New products—existing markets
> New products—new markets
>
> *or*
>
> Unit sales by area
> Unit sales by product
> Unit sales by customer
>
> *or*
>
> Pound (cash) sales of product A
> Pound (cash) sales of product B
> Pound (cash) sales of product C
>
> *or*
>
> Sales of product A
> Gross margin product A
> Profitability product A

One of these four sets or some combination of them would suit most situations. The set of effectiveness standards chosen is that which best covers the total job in output terms.

The effectiveness area 'profit' may be broken down into these effectiveness standards:

> Gross profit
> Net profit
> Profit by line

Profit by territory
Profit as a per cent of sales
Profit as a per cent of capital
Rate of profit change

In much the same way material processing could be divided into quality standards and scrap level; while safety could be divided into accident frequency and time lost.

Notice that all of the effectiveness standards are still outputs.

3.1.4 *Objectives*

Objectives are essentially specific effectiveness standards. They have time limits and numerical values attached to them. Thus for the effectiveness area 'sales' we have seen that one effectiveness standard might be £ sales of product A. The associated objective might then be 'increase sales of product A by £15,000 for the period 1st January – 31st December, 1971'.

A complete example linking effectiveness areas, effectiveness standards and objectives follows.

3.2 The concepts related

The concepts are related in this way:

Effectiveness area
Product A

Effectiveness standards
Sales increase in £ Product A
Gross margin increase in per cent Product A
Profitability increase per unit in £ Product A

Objectives
1 Increase sales of product A to £400,000
during. . . .

2 Increase gross margin of product A to 22 per cent by decreasing distribution cost to £1·10 per unit during. . . .

3 Increase profitability of product A to £0·22 during. . . .

For each effectiveness standard there is usually one objective, as shown in the example above.

3.3 The importance of these concepts

These concepts of managerial effectiveness, effectiveness areas, effectiveness standards, and objectives have an enormous importance to the organisation in many ways. Each is of course linked to each of the others but each is also linked to some important aspect of the organisation or its operation.

Concept	*Directly related to*
MANAGERIAL EFFECTIVENESS —The importance placed on outputs	ORGANISATION PHILOSOPHY —Managerial effectiveness can be a clear statement of what an organisation thinks is really important.
EFFECTIVENESS AREAS	SYSTEM DESIGN —What kind of position outputs do we have and want and what structure is best to obtain them?
EFFECTIVENESS STANDARDS —What are the outputs of particular positions	JOB SPECIFICATIONS —What kind of manager is required? MANAGER SELECTION —Is this the man we want?

TRAINING PLANS
—What kind of training is
needed for performance
in the position?

JOB EVALUATION
—How much should we
pay?

OBJECTIVES
—and degree to which
met

CORPORATE STRATEGY
—Do objectives serve to aid
the corporate strategy?

MANAGERIAL APPRAISAL
—How well does the mana-
ger perform?

COACHING
—Based on how he has
performed – in what does
he need personal assis-
tance?

CAREER PLANNING
—What is the best succes-
sion of positions for each
manager?

BUDGETS
—How do possible levels of
budgets and objectives
relate?

MANAGERIAL INVENTORY
—What is our quality and
experience level?

3.4 Functional areas related to effectiveness areas

As an aid to managers who wish to think about their effectiveness areas, here are sets of effectiveness areas usually associated
with specific functions. There is a great deal of overlap however
and several of those listed under 'production' for instance

would apply equally to several other functions. The functions covered are:

> Production
> Material
> Marketing
> Personnel
> Finance – Accounting
> Supply

3.4.1 *Production effectiveness areas*
Production effectiveness areas include:

> Quality
> Quantity
> Timing
> Scrap
> Rejects
> Inventory
> Labour costs
> Material costs
> Safety
> Machinery utilisation

and the associated material effectiveness areas.

3.4.2 *Material effectiveness areas*
Material effectiveness areas include:

> Unit cost reductions
> Unit cost handling
> Scrap
> Rejects
> Inventory level
> Inventory ratio
> Model change time

The management of manufacturing processes generally is assisted greatly by MBO.

3.4.3 *Marketing effectiveness areas*

> Sales
> Margins
> Costs
> New markets
> New customers
> Marketing strategy
> Market research
> Marketing plans
> Market penetration
> Distribution

While all functional areas are suitable for MBO implementation, there is little doubt that marketing is one of the easiest functional areas in which to draft effectiveness areas.

3.4.4 *Personnel effectiveness areas*

> Selection
> Management succession
> Wage and salary equity
> Personnel policy
> Management information
> Union – management relations
> Contract terms
> Safety
> Behaviour change
> Training

One issue that has to be sorted out with labour effectiveness areas is just whose responsibility they are. There is sometimes some confusion about whether certain of the labour effectiveness areas are the responsibility of the personnel department or whether that department's role is limited to simply collecting the data and providing advice. The answer depends on who really approves the appropriate policies and who really controls the reward and punishment system associated with the policy implementation.

3.4.5 *Finance – accounting effectiveness areas*

> Cost of capital
> Capital availability
> Statutory information
> Management information
> Data processing
> Accounts receivable
> Cost effectiveness
> Annual report
> Audit
> Disbursements

3.4.6 *Supply effectiveness areas*

> Acquisition cost
> Processing cost
> Production cost
> Distribution cost
> Number
> Average size
> Damage claims
> Customer complaints
> Missed delivery dates
> Back-order level

Supply effectiveness areas are of interest to both marketing and distribution. The first four effectiveness areas listed form a set, and it is often very useful to identify and separate these four cost elements.

3.5 Where from here?

Clearly every management position has effectiveness areas associated with it. Chapter 5 shows how to establish them.

To make it easy to start, however, there are some areas common to all, or most, positions and we can deal with those first.

New concepts introduced – Chapter 3

EFFECTIVENESS AREAS (EA):
General output requirements of a managerial position.

EFFECTIVENESS STANDARDS (ES):
Specific output requirements and measurement criteria of a managerial position.

OBJECTIVES (O):
Effectiveness standards which are as specific, as time bounded and as measurable as possible.

4 Common Effectiveness Areas

Innovation is part of every manager's job.

The single-minded pursuit of an objective means that a manager has learned the name of the game, not the spirit of it.

Every manager has a responsibility for his co-workers' effectiveness.

All management positions, no matter how different, do have some common effectiveness areas. 'Common effectiveness areas' are those which may be, and usually are, associated with every management position. The other areas which are specific to particular management positions are called 'specific areas' – all that have been referred to in this book to so far have been of this type.

4.1 Common effectiveness areas

These are:

> SUBORDINATE effectiveness area
> INNOVATIVE effectiveness area
> PROJECT effectiveness area
> DEVELOPMENT effectiveness area
> SYSTEMS effectiveness area
> CO-WORKER effectiveness area

This chapter will explain each of these common effectiveness areas and give illustrative effectiveness standards and objectives for them. Not all of the common effectiveness areas meet the stern tests of output and completely objective measurement suggested for the specific effectiveness areas. They do not because several of the common effectiveness areas are, by their very nature, designed simply to ensure organisational continuity rather than to achieve the outputs of particular positions.

4.1.1 *Subordinate effectiveness area*

Every management position which has positions subordinate to it needs to have 'subordinate effectiveness' as an effectiveness area. This effectiveness area serves to focus sharply on the true relationship needed between superior and subordinate. It can be broken down into two effectiveness standards, the first referring to setting objectives for the forthcoming year and the second to meeting them for the current year. These two standards taken together force recognition of the fact that a manager is responsible to his superior for the performance of subordinates. He can fulfil this responsibility in any way he wants. The standards say nothing about how. He will have to use his skills in motivation, coaching, direct assistance, aid in planning or organising, resource allocation and so on, depending upon the circumstances.

An associated objective could be worded along these lines: 'Each subordinate to establish measurable objectives by 15th August, 1971, which are agreed to by those concerned, and which align horizontally and vertically.' The term 'align' in the objectives refers to the meshing of objectives both across and up and down so that, as a simple example, the production department plans to make what the marketing department plans to sell. The idea here is that the quality measures are having the objectives approved and tested for a good fit with those of other positions in the organisation. The time measure is that the objectives would be approved some three months prior to the beginning of the year to which they apply. The objective is specific in that it clearly refers to effectiveness areas and objectives and to all subordinates. Such objectives as these substitute for customary objectives concerning motivation, control, relationships and delegation which do not get to the heart of the matter which is effectiveness.

Unnecessary emphasis is sometimes used in the wording of objectives concerning subordinates:

> 'To *ensure* that subordinates will achieve. . . .'
> 'To *motivate* subordinates to achieve. . . .'

All these sound terribly powerful and dynamic but add nothing.

4.1.2 *Innovative effectiveness area*

The 'innovative effectiveness' area refers to doing something new on one's own initiative. It does not refer to doing things better or to implementing innovations which others propose.

The mere existence of this as a common effectiveness area results in annual questioning of 'the way we are doing things now'. Associated effectiveness standards might concern proposal or implementation:

> 'Propose X new'
> 'Introduce X new'

If proposing new products was not normally part of one's job the following objective might apply: 'DUR 1972 propose five new products to the product committee, each with a four-year sales potential of £x and have one accepted for trial testing'. This objective is, though, somewhat grand for a manager who does not have innovation as his full time job. More realistic objectives may relate to innovations in methods or procedures.

4.1.3 *Project effectiveness area*

Another common effectiveness area is 'project effectiveness'. Projects concern those things which are not a normal part of the job and which are not innovations to the existing job. They most usually arise from an assignment from the manager's superior. Its associated standards refer to projects which are usually of a 'one-shot' nature. They may refer to such things as:

> Project committee membership
> Conversion of paper files to microfilm
> Appraisal of any system
> Redesign of any system
> Initiation of any system
> Conducting special investigations
> Temporary assignment to other departments

Such standards then usually refer to such things as feasibility studies and trial applications of as yet untested new systems.

41

The objectives based on the standards may form the basis of project-team problem solving and are usually self-cancelling once-the objective is achieved. Special objectives often have a lower priority than others, and, of course, they may vary widely from year to year.

4.1.4 *Development effectiveness area*
'Development effectiveness' refers to preparing to meet the objectives of the position. Effectiveness standards may include:

> Human skills acquisition
> Technical skill acquisition
> Conceptual skill acquisition
> Work habit modification

There may be only a single objective in a particular year which could be worded along these lines: 'Prepare myself DUR 1972 to be able to meet my objectives now established and those which will probably be established during the next x years.' The associated activities could be any of:

> Making a time budget
> Reading specific management books
> Obtaining practice in using PERT diagrams for objectives
> Seminar participation
> Visits
> Conference attendance

All managers would wish to set at least one objective in this area each year. If they do not it is unlikely that they are improving their overall capacity at the rate they could. On the other hand, overemphasis on this kind of thing, and some managers do just this, simply indicates a man who hasn't got a job. He develops himself and not the business.

Many of these developmental objectives have a strong input rather than output flavour but should be made as output orientated as possible. For instance, concerning training, not 'attend a five day PERT network seminar'; but, 'be able to use PERT for at least two of my objectives'; or better 'use PERT for at least two of my objectives'.

4.1.5 *Systems effectiveness area*

A manager is part of a system. If the system does not work, the achievement or lack of achievement of his objectives is inconsequential. Clearly, all managers have a responsibility to respond to the structure of the system of which their position is an integral part. Some managers carry it too far, and believe that an ideal manager in all circumstances is the bureaucrat who is interested first in maintaining the system.

Management by objectives is a way of managing an organisation; it is not a game to win. The single-minded pursuit of an objective while not also considering the firm as a system means only that a manager has learned the name of the game, not the spirit of it.

Systems effectiveness is needed as a common effectiveness area. It relates to a manager's responsibility to see that his position and unit fit well into the broader scheme of budgets and procedures. A budget is a device for making an organisation work as designed. In the same way so are standard operating procedures. An associated objective might be worded: 'To maintain the company budget, procedural, and administrative control systems.'

'Budget' as an associated effectiveness standard should not be included, of course, if the manager has no budget responsibility. Nor if the manager is also a revenue centre when a 'margin' or 'cost per pound received' specific effectiveness standard can be used instead. Nor if the budget is so constructed as to have only one to three key items, in which case it is often a good idea to express the objectives in terms of these instead.

4.1.6 *Co-worker effectiveness area*

'Co-worker effectiveness' is a common effectiveness area only for those who have co-workers. The common area exists to emphasise the role of the manager as an external representative of his department. It gives recognition to the essential linking needed for a firm's sub-parts if organisational effectiveness is to be achieved.

An associated objective might be worded along the lines of: 'In the opinion of each co-worker, to have done nothing to inhibit his managerial effectiveness.' Some managers prefer to word this positively as: 'In the opinion of each co-worker, to have aided him in achieving his managerial effectiveness.' While the measurement method is a trifle subjective the method itself is clear – you ask them.

Some managers shy away from this common effectiveness area with a variety of excuses. It is sometimes because they have been trained too well to look upward and downward in the organisation, and not across.

4.2 Do all apply?

Do all the common effectiveness areas apply to all management positions? The rule is, 'when in doubt try to make them apply'. One MBO specialist in a firm which had a low rate of new product launches and low creativity suggested initially that the 'innovative effectiveness' area could not generally apply. He was trapped by the firm he was in. For the very reason it appeared to be difficult naturally suggested its use there. If a common area is seen not to apply it is best to take a close look at the reasons given. They may be obvious and correct. On the other hand they may be neither. When possible, then, all managers should attempt to apply all the common areas to their position.

4.3 Personal effectiveness

Individual managers will naturally have their own personal objectives, relating perhaps to salary and advancement. The associated effectiveness area is personal effectiveness. This area is the manager's own business, and, while it can be subjected to the same rigour as other areas, it is not part of the formal MBO programme, which is concerned solely with managerial effectiveness, not personal effectiveness.

4.4 Common effectiveness areas and the functions of management

Many management writers define what they see as the functions of management. Among the best known are:

VIEWS OF THE FUNCTIONS OF MANAGEMENT

Luther & Gulick (1937)	Newman & Summer (1961)	Koontz & O'Donnell (1964)	Dale (1965)
Planning	Planning	Planning	Planning
Organising	Organising	Organising	Organising
Staffing		Staffing	Staffing
Directing	Leading	Direction	Direction
Co-ordinating			
Reporting	Controlling	Control	Control
	Measuring		
			Innovation
			Representation

These have all been useful lists and there is a fairly high degree of agreement among them. The list Effective MBO would propose is however different and it relates directly to the common effectiveness areas. The functions are:

Objectives
Planning
Subordinates

45

Innovation
Systems
Co-workers

The first is setting objectives and the next is planning. These two include most of the functions of management proposed by other authors, particularly the functions of organization, staffing, direction, control, co-ordination. The next four functions – subordinates, innovation, systems and co-workers are all common effectiveness areas. The two common effectiveness areas omitted are project and development as they are of an individual nature.

The common responsibilities of management have now been outlined, so it is time to turn to the specific ones.

New concepts introduced – Chapter 4

COMMON EFFECTIVENESS AREAS (CEA):
Those effectiveness areas which may be and usually are associated with all managerial positions.

CO-WORKER EFFECTIVENESS AREA:
A common effectiveness area concerned with the effectiveness of a manager's co-workers.

DEVELOPMENT EFFECTIVENESS AREA:
A common effectiveness area concerned with a manager's preparation to meet his objectives.

INNOVATIVE EFFECTIVENESS AREA:
A common effectiveness area concerned with a manager's innovations.

PROJECT EFFECTIVENESS AREA:
A common effectiveness area concerned with a manager's special projects.

SUBORDINATE EFFECTIVENESS AREA:

A common effectiveness area concerned with the effectiveness of a manager's subordinates.

SYSTEMS EFFECTIVENESS AREA:

A common effectiveness area concerned with a manager's maintenance of budget, procedural and administrative control systems.

5 How to Establish Effectiveness Areas

First ask: Why is the position needed at all?

The effectiveness areas of a top man position are highly flexible.

If a manager can create a subordinate and assign him any effectiveness areas then the manager's job is fully flexible and he can make it what he will.

Industry has no place for a staff specialist who does not himself create consultative conditions.

A government trade commissioner had a time-weighted set of objectives which called for 15 per cent of his time on marketing and 85 per cent on reporting and administration. Sad but true.

The purpose of this and the next two chapters is to show how to establish specific effectiveness areas for a unit or department and for all positions in it.

For simplicity this chapter will deal with the effectiveness areas of managers as heads of units and will make no particular distinction between the effectiveness areas of a unit and of the manager who heads it. This distinction will be made in Chapter 7.

Every necessary managerial position has effectiveness areas associated with it. They may not be written or even known but they are always there. These are the general areas which define the true function of the position in the organisation. The process of identifying them has cured numerous management ills simply because the true reason for each position is investigated, discussed, and ultimately agreed by the manager himself and his superior.

5.1 Illustrative unit/position effectiveness areas

What follows then is a further aid to managers who wish to draft an initial set of effectiveness areas for their units and positions. Sets of effectiveness areas are given for many different positions, grouped broadly by functional area, position in the organisation, or type of organisation. One thing can be said with certainty about them. It is highly unlikely that any will fit a particular unit or position perfectly. While most are actual examples, companies differ enormously in what they mean by a particular position title. In addition, the titles of subordinate positions are not given and, most important, the locus of the real authority is not specified. Managers should use these only as a starting point in thinking about their job.

These examples are grouped as follows:

> Top man
> Knowledge workers
> Consultants
> Government
> Production
> Engineering
> Finance and accounting
> Public relations
> Marketing and sales

5.1.1 *Effectiveness areas – top man*

The effectiveness areas of a top-man position are highly flexible. They differ from one firm to another and from one top man to another, and they change for a top man over the length of time during which he grows into his job and comes to trust his subordinates more or builds the organisation around his preferred style.

This managing director of a large firm in Australia had a big-picture view of his job. He saw himself very much as a strategist.

Managing Director A
Corporate strategy
Company organisation
Management objectives
Management development
Employment of capital
Return on capital

The top man of a smaller firm of 700 employees, with little senior management below him, saw his effectiveness areas as:

Managing Director B
Yield on capital
Commodity profitability
Growth of established lines
Administrative costs
Product innovation
Long term planning
Organisation flexibility
Management succession
Trade relations
Government relations

In a larger firm or one with additional senior management, many of these areas would go to a subordinate.

The top manager of a small selling agent was naturally much more marketing and sales-oriented:

Manager of a Selling Agent
Profit on capital employed
Profit on sales
Sales with capital employed
Sales-to-stocks ratio
Costs of sales
Sales-to-promotion ratio
Market leadership
New markets

The top man, administratively, in a university of 2,000 students saw these as his areas:

> *University Vice President – Administrative*
> Provision of basic services
> Student faculty ratio
> Space utilisation system
> Cost per student
> Administrative percentage
> Academic budget allocation formula
> Organisational structure
> Financial information

He had a great deal of authority but did not get involved directly in areas of teaching or curriculum.

Compare these relatively clean and position-centred statements of areas with one of the few other published top man sets, for a large firm. This set of areas says in effect that the top man does the job of all of his subordinates. This invalid point of view will be dealt with in the next chapter.

Top man

To study the market for products and decide where to attack it

To determine the specification of new products, and to sell them

To design, make, and distribute products

To know where the revenue is to come from, where the expenditure is to go, and what the resultant profit should be

To ensure the high morale of and secure employment for, employees

To ensure the satisfaction of distributors and consumers

To ensure that the Company carries out its responsibilities to the community

5.1.2 *Effectiveness areas – Knowledge workers*

There are two kinds of statements which fit a variety of knowledge workers who have no power. One is for staff specialists in general and the other is for faculty members. This set, disarmingly simple, is capable of measurement if the associated objectives are worded correctly.

> *Staff specialist – General*
> Personal competence
> Consulted in area of competence
> Advice accepted
> Advice acceptance leads to improvement

The four areas in turn state that the specialist must be competent and that part of his job is to see that he is. The second area puts responsibility upon the specialist, not the manager, to see that he is consulted. Too many staff specialists, like some university professors, see themselves as an information reservoir with no responsibility to provide a tapping facility, which is usually so sorely needed. Staff specialists, more than managers, have the opportunity so to develop a relationship that their advice is sought when appropriate. Industry has no place for the staff specialist who does not himself create consultative conditions. The job must also include a degree of advice acceptance and of improvement leading from this.

The Effective MBO method does not agree with this statement from an MBO text:

> 'Setting specific, quantitative objectives for many staff positions is particularly troublesome for many companies. Traditionally, the line does, the staff helps. In many firms, this distinction is being softened almost to the point of obliteration as the work of the staff functions becomes more crucial to business success. Still, the nature of staff work is often hard to state in measurable terms. The staff proposes courses of action for the line to act upon. The staff studies situations to advise the line on what to do. The specific results often depend upon what the line does and are not under the direct control of the staff specialists and managers.'

Another kind of knowledge worker is the university lecturer. While often uncomfortable about the whole notion of academic effectiveness, he has these as his effectiveness areas:

> *Faculty member*
> Knowledge storage
> Knowledge retrieval
> Knowledge distribution
> Knowledge expansion

This set would include 90 to 100 per cent of every faculty member's job. Some faculty members like to add 'student relations' not recognising that this is an input to the broader purposes of the university.

A research and development manager's set of effectiveness areas might be:

> *Research and Development Manager*
> New product innovation
> Existing product development
> Patent protection
> Corporate innovative reputation

It would be likely that the first two items would be broken down into several objectives, while the last one, in some firms, would not be considered important.

5.1.3 *Effectiveness areas – Consultants*
Business consultants are usually knowledge workers who operate on a contract basis. A general set of effectiveness areas for a consultant is:

> *Consultant*
> Time utilisation
> Meet contract terms
> Client effectiveness

While the manager of the consultant might have these:

> *Branch Manager – Consulting firm*
> Profit
> Sales
> Business mix
> Quality of service
> Costs
> Sales expansion
> Consultant quality

5.1.4 *Effectiveness areas – Government in Canada*

Positions in government pose no inherent problem for MBO implementation. The difficulty arises when the position has no real authority and the incumbent is really a clerk, or when the incumbent is so busy filing reports on what he is doing that he does little else.

A Government Trade Commissioner had a time-weighted set of objectives. They asked him to spend 15 per cent of his time on marketing and 85 per cent of his time on reporting and administration. Sad but true.

The director of a National Government Communication Centre had these as his effectiveness areas:

> *Director – National Government*
> *Communication Centre*
> Messages handled
> Transmission delay
> Security
> Error rate
> Peak-load facility

He had no control over the message input, but he could influence staff size over time.

A Deputy Minister of Agriculture had these as his effectiveness areas:

> *Deputy Minister of Agriculture*
> Agricultural development
> Agricultural productivity
> Public relations crisis management
> Return on budget
> Legislation innovation

They reveal an imaginative view of his job. All the associated objectives were measurable and related primarily to his efforts.

The single employee of a farm loan board had these effectiveness areas:

> *Farm Loan Board Manager*
> Loan losses
> Loan arrears
> Loan outstanding
> Legislation innovations
> Loan leverage
> Private-lending availability

These again show, in the last three areas, a broad view of his job. The last area is particularly significant. Part of the job was to eliminate the need for it.

The Crop Director of a Canadian province also had an easily measurable set of outputs:

> *Crop Director*
> Tobacco acreage
> Crop insurance coverage
> Noxious weeds
> Soil and feed sample requests
> Seed production
> Research output
> Pesticide residue de-emphasis
> Land use planning
> Farmer knowledge

In government, as long as a job exists to be done and as long as the manager has some authority and resources, a set of effectiveness areas based on outputs may be constructed.

5.1.5 *Effectiveness areas – Production*
Production, together with marketing, tends to be the easiest function for which to form effectiveness areas, and objectives and statements of them abound in the literature.

The effectiveness areas can vary very much from position to position, however, depending on such things as whether or not:

> Continuous-flow process is used
> Plant has autonomy over policy, especially personnel
> Structure at the top is flat or tall
> Models change frequently

A mill superintendent had this set of effectiveness areas:

> *Logging Mill Superintendent*
> Production level
> Production cost
> Production quality
> Labour safety

While a plant manager in another firm had this set:

> *Plant Manager*
> Production level
> Production cost
> Production quality
> Labour safety
> Inventory control
> Machine and space utilisation
> Delivery times

Notice that the plant manager had the complete set of the logging mill superintendent plus three additional areas. The mill superintendent had one simple process, he had no responsibility for supply, and the logs took a fixed time to process. The plant manager, on the other hand, had twenty different products to produce and responsibility for raw material supply, and he could delay producing some products to maximise machine and space utilisation.

The effectiveness areas for quality control depend much on whether the position involved is simply advisory or not. If a quality control manager has fairly broad authority, his effectiveness areas could be:

> *Quality Control Manager*
> Quality standards
> Quality level
> Quality control cost
> Quality control methods

If he has little authority his effectiveness areas would reflect that his job was to detect and report deviations quickly and accurately at low cost.

5.1.6 *Effectiveness areas – Engineering*
A power system engineering manager had these effectiveness areas:

> *Power System Engineering Manager*
> Design of power systems
> Protection of power systems
> Design of generation plant
> Construction of generation plant
> Design of transmission system
> Construction of transmission system
> Operation of thermal plant

and a mechanical engineering manager had these:

> *Mechanical Engineering Manager*
> Plant installations
> Design of manufactured equipment
> Machinery specifications

5.1.7 *Effectiveness areas – Finance and Accounting*

Accountants can have serious problems in defining their effectiveness areas. Their training has essentially been in information collection and storage. Some of them think their job is done when books or figures are neat, well stored, and accurately counted. But this is not their real job. Their real job, of course, is facilitating information retrieval, not facilitating information storage.

A typical set of effectiveness areas for an accountant is:

> *Accountant*
> Management information
> Statutory information
> Forecasting
> Control

Notice that the first and second effectiveness areas are designed to separate clearly the responsibility imposed by government legislation and that imposed by firm profitability.

A vice president – finance had this set of effectiveness areas:

> *Vice President – Finance*
> Capital inflow
> Finance of acquisitions
> Legal aspects of acquisitions
> Cost of capital
> Internal financial information
> Underwriter relationships
> Government financial relationships

Notice the absence of overlap between the two sets of effectiveness areas.

5.1.8 *Effectiveness areas – Public Relations*

As with many such staff jobs the important question to ask about the position of public relations director is, Who really has the power? It may be that the managing director approves all press notices, that no public relations policy exists, and that the public relations director simply responds to his in-basket rather than exercising initiative over policy or programmes. He may be a clerk.

One public relations manager of an airline had this set of effectiveness areas:

> *Public Relations Manager*
> Corporate information availability
> Corporate image
> Column inches obtained
> Public relations crisis management

The last item, for him, was a particularly important measure. When a plane crashes, what is and what is not done or 'managed' in the next twenty-four hours can be crucial to the airline.

5.1.9 *Effectiveness areas – Marketing and Sales*

A United States sales manager of a large Canadian firm had these as his effectiveness areas:

> *Manager – United States Sales*
> Profit
> Sales
> Accounts receivable
> Inventory turnover
> Image
> Marketing strategy
> New-product sales
> New-product proposals

The profit and sales areas are usually present. Accounts receivable was important owing to the few very large accounts involved and the very short cycle from raw material purchase to product. Inventory turnover was important owing to the short shelf life of the product. Image was in because the company had previously entered and withdrawn from the United States market three times and had left behind poor trade relations. This manager proposed to spend 25 per cent of his time on this area and to contract for a quarterly survey among all major customers. New product sales was separated from sales simply to give it more importance while new product proposals was put in owing to the newness of the market to the vice president – marketing who wanted to increase the quantity of United States style products.

A marketing manager of a New Zealand firm had these effectiveness areas:

Marketing Manager
Revenue
Margins
Sales policies
Distribution
Product innovation
Legislation
Manpower development
Consumer product image
Market intelligence

A basic set which applies to most marketing managers is:

Marketing Manager
Brand strategy
Advertising strategy
Market penetration policy
Marketing margin

While a sales manager typically has something like:

> *Sales Manager*
> Sales policies
> Sales levels
> Sales costs
> Line profitability

5.2 Guide for identifying and testing specific effectiveness areas

Here is a simple list of questions for a manager to ask himself. He should then be able to develop an initial list of effectiveness areas to test on his superior and his co-workers. There is much overlap in the list. All that the questions really ask is – What is the job? But they ask it in different ways. Some managers find that ideas are triggered when the question is asked in one way and some when it is given another way:

> What is the position's unique contribution?
> Why is the position needed at all?
> What would change if the position were eliminated?
> What changes if I am highly effective in the position?
> How would I know, with no one telling me, when I am performing effectively?
> Where does asking 'Why?' lead?
> What authority does the position really have?
> What can the position most easily improve?
> What does the job description and the organisational manual say?
> What is the biggest external change made that affected the position?
> How do I spend my time? How would I like to spend it?
> What would I be most likely to concentrate on over two or three years if I wanted to make the greatest improvement in my unit? In my superior's unit? In the organisation as a whole?

5.2.1 *Do effectiveness areas cover the whole job?*

One of the more interesting differences of approach of writers of MBO books is in the percentage of the job that they believe should be covered by effectiveness areas. One writer says: 'The key results analysis probably covers only the 15 per cent of his total tasks which are vital and leaves him great discretion in the others.'

Advocates of the effective MBO method, on the other hand, believe that effectiveness areas, and therefore objectives, must cover 100 per cent of the job. To some extent this is facilitated by the 'common areas' concept.

5.2.2 *How many effectiveness areas?*

The number of effectiveness areas a manager has depends more on how he sees his job than on what his job is. It is quite possible for two men in identical positions to have a different number of areas. A few managers report that they work effectively with up to fifteen effectiveness areas while others work effectively with only one, though usually with many associated objectives. While the number of effectiveness areas must always depend on the manager himself, a range of three to seven or eight is normal, plus the common effectiveness areas normally associated with any managerial position.

5.2.3 *Rules for wording effectiveness areas*

There are three simple rules to follow when wording effectiveness areas. They are:

1. Use from one to four words.
2. Avoid directional indicators such as 'increase', 'maximise', 'satisfy'.
3. Avoid any quantities or timings.

These three rules help to ensure that effectiveness areas are not confused with effectiveness standards or objectives, and that organisational design rather than corporate planning is the focus.

5.2.4 *Guides for testing effectiveness areas*

Once effectiveness areas are identified, they should satisfy ten tests. These check on the adequacy of the effectiveness areas individually, collectively, and with respect to the associated positions.

Each effectiveness area should

1 Represent output, not input
2 Lead to associated objectives which are measurable
3 Be an important part of the position
4 Be within the actual limits of authority and responsibility

Effectiveness areas as a whole should

5 Represent 100 per cent of the outputs of the position
6 Not be so many as to avoid dealing with the essence of the job or so few as to make planning difficult

Effectiveness areas, with respect to the associated positions should

7 Avoid overlaps
8 Avoid underlaps
9 Align vertically
10 Align horizontally

These last four tests are the subject of Chapter 7.

5.3 The flexibility of effectiveness areas

The manager at the top of any organisational unit usually has some flexibility in the choice of the effectiveness areas he decides to associate with his own position. This freedom is very marked when he has the ability to create a subordinate and can assign part of his own work to the subordinate. Under these conditions the top man's areas are in fact fully flexible; he can make them what he wants. He could, for instance, become an 'outside' man with an emphasis on liaison with other organisational units or customers. His newly created subordinate could be the 'inside' man concerned with managing the unit. The reverse situation is equally feasible. This demonstrates clearly that, within broad limits, a manager who can create a subordinate and can design his subordinate's effectiveness areas has a very wide range of different areas which he can associate with his own job.

It is impossible to look at the effectiveness areas for a particular position in isolation. Such areas are best seen as sets of areas which link several positions together. It is quite possible then that if the set of areas for one position changes a great deal, sets of areas for other positions may change as well, and should. When setting areas, then, the question is not 'What are they?' but 'What could they best be.' Clearly MBO is intimately related to organisational design and organisational flexibility.

A plant manager after three years on the job may well decide to change the effectiveness areas he established three years earlier. He may have trained one or more subordinates to assume some of them.

The important thing is that effectiveness areas should not simply be applied to an existing organisational design and then considered to be relatively permanent; the assigning of effectiveness areas should be used as a basis for inducing organisational flexibility and seeing that it is maintained.

Effectiveness areas are usually subject to change when:

> A new manager is appointed
> Co-workers change
> A manager grows in skill
> Power and decision levels move
> MBO is implemented
> Any major organisational change occurs

It would be an unusual manager who could draft a perfect set of effectiveness areas simply after reading this chapter. Some assistance is always useful and is usually required. First the manager should draft and re-draft his effectiveness areas as he sees them. Then he should discuss his statement of them with his co-workers, his superior and an in-company MBO specialist if one is available. The more common errors in drafting effectiveness areas can be avoided by studying the examples of such errors in the next chapter.

New concepts introduced – Chapter 5

SPECIFIC EFFECTIVENESS AREAS:
> Effectiveness areas specific to particular managerial positions rather than common to all.

UNIT EFFECTIVENESS AREAS:
> The full set of effectiveness areas for a managerial position and all subordinate positions but not necessarily including the common effectiveness areas.

6 Errors in Effectiveness Areas

Effectiveness areas should not reflect an intent to safeguard resources but to optimise resource allocation.

There is an administrative accident-proneness just as serious and as obvious as physical accident-proneness.

If you cannot measure it forget it as no one will know anyway.

The most typical errors in writing effectiveness areas arise from confusing an effectiveness area with one or more of the following:

> An input area
> A worry area
> Another's area
> A non-measurable area
> A time area

6.1 Input area

The most common error in writing effectiveness areas is in producing input areas. An input area is an incorrect statement of an effectiveness area which is based on activities or inputs rather than results or outputs.

6.1.1 *Examples*
The Director of Agricultural Extension. A director of agricultural extension work with a staff of about forty initially established these as his effectiveness areas:

> *First attempt*
> 1 Fill staff positions adequately
> 2 Staff competence

3 Professional staff turnover
4 Organise and develop extension programme
5 Promote activity in farm youth clubs
6 Conduct studies and prepare reports
7 Supervise loan grants to farmers

After becoming acquainted with MBO, and particularly with methods of establishing effectiveness areas, he decided that this attempt needed improvement. In particular, he saw that he was taking no responsibility for change, and that he was focusing on inputs, not outputs. His proposed effectiveness areas indicated a low-level bureaucratic view of his job. Like many of those employed by government, he greatly over emphasised staffing, programmes, and report writing. All of these are important, of course, but they do not relate directly to the basic function of the position.

The director made a second attempt at setting his effectiveness areas.

Second attempt
8 Net farm income
9 Percentage of commercial farmers
10 High value crop acreage
11 Average number of livestock

This second attempt very clearly focuses on an end result, on output, not input. In discussion, however, he found that to some extent he had gone too far the other way. He could not make 'net farm income' an effectiveness area, as so many factors affected it over which he had no control, including such things as government policy and farm board decisions. His third attempt was somewhere between the first and second attempts.

Third attempt
12 Average farm acreage
13 Secure farm loans
14 High value crop acreage
15 Average number of livestock
16 Farmer knowledge

Areas 10 (high value crop acreage) and 11 (average number of livestock) remain. Area 8 (net farm income) was removed. Two of the director's major resources, used to help increase net farm income, were loans to farmers and educational staff, programmes, and facilities. The director decided to make these into effectiveness areas largely to replace 'net farm income'. His final areas focused him on ends, not means, on what he had to achieve, not what he did. The objectives associated with all of these effectiveness areas were easily measurable and all were clearly output not input.

In a letter to the author, the director wrote,

'Number 1 was my first attempt at setting these down. Number 2 represented my first change. Number 3 is what I thought was a refinement on the second. I am still not completely satisfied with these and I will now discuss these at some length with my superior in order to arrive at what we both feel is the best set of effectiveness areas for my position. The problem that I faced initially in preparing them was that I am in a position of directing a number of programme areas, and a lot of the decisions I make are with reference to staffing, budgeting, personnel and additions to programmes. This led me to lose sight of what I was actually supposed to accomplish.'

Too many attempts to set effectiveness areas fall into one of the two traps illustrated by this director's first and second attempts. Either they focus on inputs and turn managers into bureaucrats, or they deal with uncontrollable outputs and so become predictions, dreams, or simply part of another manager's job.

The Training Officer. While many initial attempts to set effectiveness areas turn out to be a list of activities instead, many attempts can go in the other direction, so that everyone appears to think he is heading a profit centre. Of any proposed effectiveness area the question should be asked, 'Why is this being done?' or 'Why is this important?' For example, a training manager might go through this kind of process. He is first asked what his most important area is. To which he might reply: 'To design a management development programme.' When asked 'Why?' he replies, 'To put on courses for managers.' When again asked 'Why?' he replies, 'To increase managerial skill in problem solving.' When again asked 'Why?' he replies, 'To improve the quality of managerial decisions.' To yet another 'Why?' he replies 'To improve profit performance.' The correct area for this training manager would probably be 'To increase managerial skill in problem solving.' It cannot be 'To improve the quality of managerial decisions' or 'To improve profit performance', as these are both influenced by many factors over which the training manager has no control as he has no authority. On the other hand, the areas cannot be simply 'Programme design' or 'Putting on courses', which are clearly inputs. The sole objective of industrial training is to change behaviour. The effectiveness areas and the objectives of a training manager must reflect this.

The Senior Public Servant. A senior public servant said he was using MBO. He said that one of his effectiveness areas was 'letter answering' and that the associated objective was to answer all letters within two days. When he hears things like this, an MBO specialist should try to be participative and supportive and say, 'How nice'. Here was a perfect example of an emphasis on inputs, not outputs, on apparent effectiveness, not managerial effectiveness. He was asked the key question, 'Why do you want to answer all letters within two days?' and he replied, 'To improve our service to clients.' He was asked again, 'Why?' and still again 'Why?' until he ended up with seeing his job linked to increasing national income. One could say that his real job was to increase national income, but here we are going off the other end of the output scale, as this public servant obviously had no control over many decisions affecting national income. His real effectiveness areas were somewhere between.

Notice that all three of the examples just given refer to administrative rather than manufacturing or sales positions. These were chosen deliberately, as it is popularly believed that it is not possible to view such positions from an output point of view. This is clearly incorrect.

6.1.2 *Inputs gone wild*

Here are the proposed effectiveness areas, though called by another name, of three staff positions. These, together with the areas for other positions, were published and widely distributed by a consulting firm to demonstrate the type of work they did. They demonstrated it only too well.

Training Officer

For administering the training of all personnel in operator or technical or managerial skills

For formulating training methods

For maintaining training records

For advising on methods of meeting the requirements of the Industry's Training Board and for liaison with that Board

For reviewing all developments in training techniques and for applying them when suitable to the Company's requirements

Security Officer

For maintaining a fire watch and security team

For carrying out periodic searches to combat pilfering

For advising on the methods or procedures to combat industrial espionage

For liaison with the police in cases of prosecution for security offences

Safety Officer

For ensuring that the Company meets statutory requirements for the safety of personnel

For carrying out safety checks on any equipment or operation and advising the management of the department on the action required to eliminate any hazards

For providing safety training and promoting safety consciousness

Or, believe it or not, a firm in the United States similarly published the following objectives as models, published in turn by the American Management Association.

Personnel Manager

Fix responsibility: to fix responsibility for each function.

Delegate authority commensurate with responsibility: to delegate authority and accountability commensurate with responsibility, and to recognise that the three are inseparable.

Follow organisational lines: individuals shall not circumvent the lines of authority.

Give each employee one administrative supervisor: to give each employee only one administrative supervisor.

Recognise the individual: to handle all Company-employee relationships with understanding, honesty, and courtesy, recognising the employee's individuality and dignity.

Outside interests: to respect the rights of employees to engage in activities outside of their employment, which may be private or public in nature and (shall) in no way conflict with or reflect unfavourably upon the Company and/or its corporate image, nor encroach upon the rights of the Company to the full services of its employees.

It would appear that the training officer was not responsible for changing behaviour, the security officer was not responsible for fire or thefts, and the safety officer was not responsible for safety levels while the personnel manager had such a mixed-up set of inputs that he was either very busy or had nothing to do.

6.1.3 Conversion of inputs to outputs

Most inputs can be converted to outputs if the position is needed at all.

Examples of inputs converted to outputs
Maintain machines to Machine availability
Coach subordinates to Subordinate effectiveness
Teach PERT   to PERT usage
Church attendance to Christian values
Farmer education   to High value crop acreage

Beware of such areas as these which usually suggest inputs:

Communication
Relationships
Liaison
Co-ordination
Staffing

6.2 Worry area

Another common error is in identifying worry areas. A *worry area* is an effectiveness area a manager shows as his own because he does not expect another manager, whose responsibility it really is, to deal with it effectively without intervention. In organisations which have grown rapidly and which have weak management development programmes the top man often proposes several worry areas among his effectiveness areas. The underlying problems may be one or more of these:

Lack of delegation
Subordinate incompetence
Confusion over where decision is actually made

At a meeting between the general manager in a public utility and all his subordinates, the general manager proposed 'labour relations' as an effectiveness area for his position; but so did the personnel director for his position. The consultant pointed out, 'If two people are responsible for the same thing, one of them is not needed – and the thing would not be done well anyway.' This duplication of an effectiveness area prompted a lengthy discussion on the lack of true delegation of the top man in certain areas. The personnel director thought he should have the effectiveness area as his own, but said he did not mind who had it as long as only one person did. The area was eventually given to the personnel director, and many underlying issues were solved when it was.

If MBO is put in without the identification and modification of problems such as worry areas it simply freezes what may already be a poorly designed organisation structure.

6.3 Another's area

A third error in writing effectiveness areas is called 'another's area'. This is an effectiveness area a manager shows as his own over which he has no control. This is distinct from a worry area in that it arises from a confusion of where the power lies rather than from a distrust of competence or interest. Such confusion can often arise if the power of the staff, or lack of it, is not clearly defined. In one Canadian firm this issue arose sharply over quality control. As it was worked out, the effectiveness areas concerning it were assigned as:

> Establish standards (Vice President Development)
> Information on conditions (Quality Control Inspector)
> Implementation (Vice President Production)

All of these deal with quality control, but all are completely different.

Decisions associated with successful products tend to move upward as those managers associated with the sound decisions get promoted. This is particularly true in marketing orientated firms. As a temporary measure this is appropriate, as new subordinate competence may not be fully developed and a poor decision may be too much risk to take. In one British

73

firm, the key decisions, concerning price and advertising percentage of a highly successful product, stayed with the man who was promoted from brand manager to marketing director. This meant that the new brand manager was really a brand planner. This gives rise to such linked positions as the following four:

> Marketing Director
> Brand Manager
> Brand Planner
> Salesman

All suggest different effectiveness areas, and a sound MBO implementation could clarify exactly what each is responsible for so that the 'another's area' problem does not arise.

6.4 Non-measurable area

The fourth error in writing effectiveness areas is the 'non-measurable area', which is an effectiveness area whose associated objective is not measurable. Whether or not the associated objective is measurable cannot always be determined simply from the wording of the area or standard itself and would have to be obtained instead from the proposed objective.

While the measurement problem can usually be solved with imagination, the cost of the measurement problem may remain. Measurement of the impact of training on behaviour necessitates many phone calls or questionnaires, and preferably a field survey. The outputs of a public relations position are hard to measure without a formal survey of some kind. In cases like this, one has to ask whether the function is important enough to have even a rough measurement of its effectiveness. If not, then eliminate the function. If so, then allocate 10 per cent of the total appropriate budget to measurement. There is too much conventional wisdom that a particular activity is a 'good thing'. Measurement is the only way to test it.

A difficult thing for some managers to accept about MBO is, 'If you cannot measure it, forget it, because no one will known anyway.' Accurate measurement is central to MBO. Without measurement, MBO cannot be implemented. Some managers initially see their job as having vague, pervasive and very long-term effects and claim that it is impossible to measure their performance by normal methods. If, when a manager learns MBO he still says his contribution is not measurable, then he:

Is in a position that is not needed

or

Has no authority to do his job

or

Is avoiding responsibility

As a simple example, good relations is often proposed as an effectiveness area. This is not measurable except by highly subjective methods. A sales manager who once proposed it said later that it was not only non-measurable but an input as well, and that he saw that his effectiveness in this area could be equally well measured by short- and long-term sales.

6.5 Time area

A *time area* represents an item on which a manager spends a great deal of his time but which is not an effectiveness area. These almost always reflect a poor organisation design where responsibilities are diffuse, a job that is too small, or a top man who is doing something simply because he likes it.

Time areas can be identified quickly, first by making a time budget, which consists of allocating a time percentage to each proposed effectiveness area, and then by asking how important the area is to the overall output of the position.

6.6 Diagnosis from incorrect effectiveness areas

It is clear that the initial drafts of effectiveness areas by the managers themselves can form an excellent basis for diagnosis of the fundamental problems in the organisation such as:

> Power concentration
> Power diffusion
> Decisions made too high up
> Decisions made too low down
> Low trust level
> Poor information system
> Lack of corporate strategy
> Lack of planning
> Control from outside the organisation
> Emphasis on maintenance, not change
> Incompetence

The identification of such things can assist an internal or external MBO specialist in planning a programme which gets the underlying problems aired and solved.

6.7 Improved effectiveness areas

Here are some examples of improved effectiveness areas which show a first and second attempt at establishing them. The first attempt was most often produced as private work during the managerial objectives seminar. The second attempt shows how these first attempts were improved after discussion with a small group at the seminar. Such before-after changes as these are typical. They demonstrate what an imperfect view many, or even most, managers have of their jobs, and how easy it is to change this view, given the appropriate method and conditions. For simplicity these examples exclude reference to the common effectiveness areas. None of the second attempts are claimed to be perfect for the job in question, and in any case this would be impossible to determine without much more information. The point being made is, simply, that the second attempt is clearly better than the first as a basis on which to set objectives.

6.7.1 *Chairman of Board*

A full-time chairman of the board of a 6,000 employee company produced these two sets of effectiveness areas:

First attempt	*Second attempt*
1 Improve value of board	7 Board decision quality
2 Assure good executive meetings	8 National corporate image
3 Provide useful counsel to company officers	9 Corporate strategy
4 Maintain effective remuneration and personnel policies for senior executives	
5 Develop good high level corporate image and public relations	
6 Initiate sound long-range planning	

The realisation that the second set was really his job led this chairman of the board to make many changes, particularly in his time allocation. He saw that 1 (Improve value of board) and 2 (Assure good executive meetings) could be replaced by 7 (Board decision quality), that 3 (Provide useful counsel to company officers) was meddling, that 4 (Maintain effective remuneration and personnel policies for senior executives) should be given to the managing director, that 5 (Develop good high-level corporate image and public relations) was his job, but on a national scale, as expressed in 8 (National corporate image), and that 6 (Initiate sound long-range planning) was best replaced by 9 (Corporate strategy).

6.7.2 *University Director of Physical Education*

A newly appointed university director of physical education with a staff of about ten produced this as his first and second attempts:

First attempt	*Second attempt*
1 Character building	7 Utilisation of facilities
2 Health	8 Readiness of facilities
3 Sports activity	9 Quality of facilities
4 Maintenance	10 Programme innovation rate
5 Staffing	
6 Future programme	11 Growth of facilities

He came to see that he could only partially influence areas 1 (Character building) and 2 (Health) and that he had no practical measuring device for the former (Character building); that 3 (Sports activity) and 4 (Maintenance) were best expressed as 7 (Utilisation of facilities) and 8 (Readiness of facilities), that 5 (Staffing) was an input and that 6 (Future programme) could be more clearly worded as 10 (Programme innovation rate). Unlike some such managers, he did have some control over the growth of his facilities and thought it appropriate to include 11 (Growth of facilities).

6.7.3 *President of 5,000-employee Food Processor*

The president of a 5,000-employee food processor initially produced a set of thirteen effectiveness areas.

First attempt	*Second attempt*
1 Profitability	14 Profitability
2 Planning	15 Planning
3 Top team quality	16 Reputation in industry
4 Profit growth	17 Company climate
5 Reputation growth	18 Customer–top management relations
6 Growth momentum	
7 Trade relations	
8 Industry relations	

First attempt

9 Government relations
10 Board and employee
   relations
11 Capital employment
12 Return on investment
13 Management succession
   plan

He decided to retain 1 (Profitability) and 2 (Planning) as
14 (Profitability) and 15 (Planning); 3 (Top team quality) he
identified as a common area; 4 (Profit growth) could be
included as a sub-objective of 14 (Profitability) by using a
longer time span; 5 (Reputation growth) was changed to 16
(Reputation in industry) – he kept this as he was a marketing-
orientated president who spent much of his time on customer
and industry visits; 6 (Growth momentum) moved to 14
(Profitability); 7 (Trade relations) moved to part of 16 (Reputation in industry); 8 (Industry relations) became more
specific as 18 (Customer–top management relations). Number
9 (Government relations) was identified as the executive vice
president's area exclusively; 10 (Board and employee relations)
he changed to 17 (Company climate); 11 (Capital employment)
and 12 (Return on investment) were given to the vice president
finance; and 13 (Management succession plan) was seen as
an area belonging to vice president personnel.

6.7.4 *Manager of Government Employment Agency*
Government officials are often perceived as being buried in
paperwork and losing sight of their real job in output terms.
Prior to an effective implementation of management by
objectives this condition is in fact prevalent. The manager of a
regional government employment agency produced what
amounted to a simple set of inputs as his first attempt. He had
been exposed to a departmental MBO programme and on
such a narrow view of his job he had based numerical
'objectives'.

	First attempt		*Second attempt*
1	Promotion of service	7	Unemployment decrease
2	Control of staff	8	Labour force upgrading
3	Capability of staff	9	Manpower forecasting
4	Availability of staff		
5	Research		
6	Planning		

About the only effectiveness area of the first attempt which he maintained was 5 (Research) but worded as 9 (Manpower forecasting), which is still somewhat on the input side but acceptable.

6.7.5 *Vice-President – Marketing*
A vice-president – marketing produced these as his first and second attempts, and only relatively minor changes were made.

	First attempt		*Second attempt*
1	Sales	7	Sales
2	Revenue	8	Ontario sales force
3	New product introduction	9	Sales costs
4	Co-ordinate sales organisa-tion in United States and Canada	10	Gross margins
5	Development of Canadian Sales Office	11	Market penetration
		12	Create United States sales organisation
6	Market penetration	13	New product sales

Area 1 (Sales) was left unchanged; 2 (Revenue) was refined to both 9 (Sales costs) and 10 (Gross margins); 3 (New product introduction) was made more on the output side by changing it to 13 (New product sales); 4 (Co-ordinate sales organisation in United States and Canada) was completely incorrect, and 12 (Create United States sales organisation) focused on what he should really do; area 6 (Market penetration) was left in as 11.

This chapter has not dealt with the relationship between the effectiveness areas of a superior and his subordinates. How these may be identified and separated is the topic of the next chapter.

New concepts introduced – Chapter 6

ANOTHER'S AREA:
An effectiveness area a manager shows as his own which is really that of another manager.

INPUT AREA:
An incorrect statement of an effectiveness area which is based on an activity rather than a result.

INPUTS:
What a manager does, or is to do, rather than what a manager achieves by doing it.

NON-MEASURABLE AREA:
An unsuitable effectiveness area as the associated objective is not measurable.

OUTPUTS:
What a manager achieves, or is to achieve, rather than what he does.

TIME AREA:
An item on which a manager spends a great deal of time but which is not an effectiveness area.

WORRY AREA:
An effectiveness area a manager shows as his own because he does not expect another manager whose area it is, to deal with it effectively without intervention.

7 How to Align Effectiveness Areas

Shared and joint objectives usually indicate poor organisational design.

If two managers are responsible for the same thing one of them is not needed.

The principle behind the system of deputies at top management level is the same as the tradesman's mate and both are usually under-employed.

I know an organisation with a hundred to one span of control. It produces a variety of complex products. It works only because each man is highly trained, the production process and each product is expertly designed and everyone obtains immediate and continuing feedback on performance. It is the London Symphony Orchestra. Why not design other organisations this way?

Early retirement is a nasty symptom of poor organisational design.

MBO implementations have led to the removal of a layer of managers.

I have never seen a personality conflict but conflict over roles or objectives is often misinterpreted.

The previous chapters have shown how to establish both specific and common effectiveness areas. Two issues of great importance however were glossed over. That is, how to separate clearly the effectiveness areas of the superior from those of his managers and from those of his unit. This clear separation of a unit's, a superior's and manager's effectiveness areas has not been dealt with directly in any MBO book written so far.

When mentioned the solution has been forced rather than cleanly resolved. This has led to the issue of effectiveness areas alignment being missed or dealt with clumsily in many MBO implementations.

7.1 Unit effectiveness areas

Unit effectiveness areas are the full set of effectiveness areas for a superior's position and for all managers' positions. These effectiveness areas can be broken down to:

> Specific effectiveness areas of the superior
> Common effectiveness areas of the superior
> Specific effectiveness areas of managers
> Common effectiveness areas of managers

By far the most important distinction to make is the difference between the specific effectiveness areas of the superior and those of the managers.

This is the important issue because if two people are responsible for the same things one of them is not needed. Major problems in such areas as delegation and planning occur when a manager sees his effectiveness areas simply as the sum of all his subordinates' effectiveness areas.

Some superiors misunderstand their job and believe that, in essence, it is to make sure subordinates do what they are supposed to do. With this view a superior's job would consist simply of his common effectiveness areas, particularly the subordinate effectiveness areas. The view, if taken to its natural conclusion, means that the sole function of all levels of management is to make sure that the workers get on with it – which is clearly incorrect. This may be true in some technologies but is not true for many. We cannot say that a superior's job is well represented by a collection of his subordinates' effectiveness areas.

7.1.1 *A Plant Manager*

During a managerial objectives seminar, a plant manager of a small, detached plant in an Australian state prepared this as an initial set of effectiveness areas.

1 Operational costs
2 Product quality
3 Production targets
4 Product development
5 Technological change
6 Return on new investment
7 Fixed asset utilisation
8 Management union relations
9 Local government relations
10 Safety

He said he knew this list was too long. He was asked to separate those areas his subordinates were responsible for, and he produced this:

My own areas
1 Operational costs
6 Return on new investment
7 Fixed asset utilisation
8 Management-union relations
9 Local government relations

My subordinates' areas
2 Product quality
3 Production targets
4 Product development
5 Technological change
10 Safety

He was then asked which of the five remaining he identified as his unique contribution rather than having simply a cause-effect relationship to the outputs of his subordinates. He saw that operational costs came directly from decisions over which his subordinates had authority. So he decided this was one of several unit effectiveness areas not related to his own position. The remaining four he decided were his unique contribution. This clear identification of his four specific areas made him realise that he had been spending too much time doing his subordinates' work.

7.1.2 *A Personnel Manager*
A personnel manager listed his effectiveness areas as: training, wage and salary administration, employment (staffing), safety and security, and industrial relations (Figure 2). He

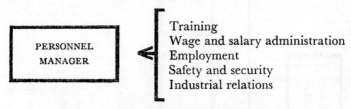

Figure 2   A personnel manager's view of his
effectiveness areas

(*At first glance this appears to be an accurate description but it is not*)

was then asked to draw for himself and his subordinates an organisation chart, to identify all the effectiveness areas starting with those of subordinates, and not to duplicate any. The result is shown in Figure 3. He ran out of effectiveness areas before he got to his own position. This is quite significant. It meant that he saw his position as having no unique responsibilities. His job, as he had defined it, was either doing his subordinates' work or making sure they did it. This was a narrow definition of his responsibility. He could see his job in broader terms than that. Surely he has more to contribute.

He was asked these questions:

What is your unique contribution?
What is the biggest thing which could go wrong?

85

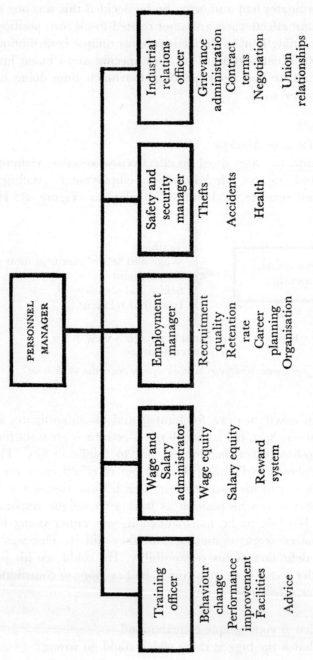

Figure 3   What is the job of the personnel manager?

(*When your subordinates share all your effectiveness areas with you, what are you left with?*)

PERSONNEL MANAGER

Training officer
- Behaviour change
- Performance improvement
- Facilities
- Advice

Wage and Salary administrator
- Wage equity
- Salary equity
- Reward system

Employment manager
- Recruitment quality
- Retention rate
- Career planning
- Organisation

Safety and security manager
- Thefts
- Accidents
- Health

Industrial relations officer
- Grievance administration
- Contract terms
- Negotiation
- Union relationships

What do, or could, you do that the managers do not because

    (*a*) they do not have the ability or experience?

    (*b*) they do not have the time?

    (*c*) they do not have the information?

Why was your position created?

What would happen if the superior's position was removed?

He came to see that his unique contribution was in the areas of:

> Personnel policy
> Working conditions
> Organisational development
> Managerial effectiveness

He could not accept full responsibility for all of these but was responsible, as any staff person, for giving acceptable advice which proves correct. Compare his first set of effectiveness areas with his revised set. They show a greatly enlarged view of the job and a preparedness to allow subordinates to get on with it.

As he had fairly experienced subordinates, he could allow them to work with full authority in their respective positions. If he lost a position in his structure or a key subordinate, he might have to take the effectiveness areas of the position concerned and add them to his own for a while.

7.1.3 *A Marketing Director*

A standard MBO text proposed Figure 4 as an example of vertical linking. While it might be true as far as it goes, it does not go very far. It does show the origin on the 10,000 units in sales but it does not give any real indication of what the top three men do – unless it is to add.

This basic diagram drawn in terms of effectiveness areas, as shown in Figure 5, is much more revealing.

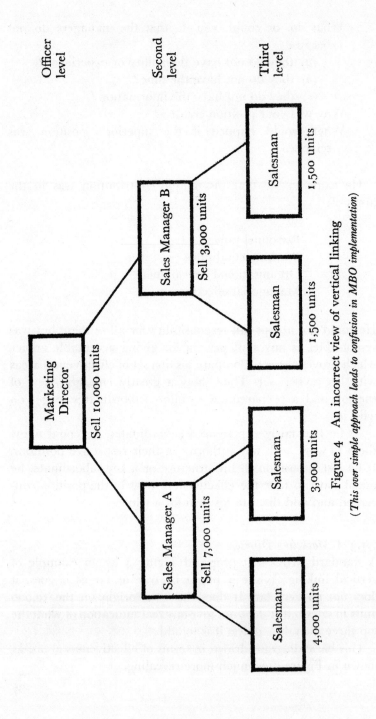

Figure 4   An incorrect view of vertical linking

(*This over simple approach leads to confusion in MBO implementation*)

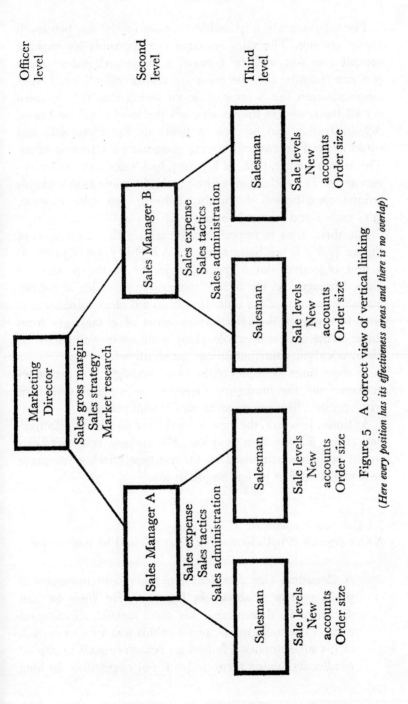

Figure 5 A correct view of vertical linking
(Here every position has its effectiveness areas and there is no overlap)

The salesmen are responsible for sales levels: the two levels above are not. The sales manager is responsible for expense control (he can add or remove a salesman), sales tactics (he can modify the direction of selling effort), and sales administration (he is responsible for seeing that the salesmen get all the resources they need), not the level above or below. Administration can be seen as being on the input side and could as well be covered by the common effectiveness areas. The sales manager, then, in Figure 4, had 'sales' as his effectiveness areas. This did not give him much of a guide as to what his unique contribution should be. Now he has sales expense, sales tactics and sales administration.

But then, who is responsible for selling the 7,000 units of Figure 4, if it is not Sales Manager A? This 7,000 objective is a unit objective, not a specific objective of the position of Sales Manager A. He is still responsible for sales of course, but only as head of his unit. If only to aid clear thinking it is wise to separate the effectiveness areas of a manager from those of his unit as a whole. This is the only way in which his own unique contribution can be identified.

In these three examples of the plant manager, the personnel manager and the marketing director, the superior ended up with specific effectiveness areas for his own position.

At times, however, the superior will have no specific effectiveness areas for his own position. His unique responsibilities would be best summarised by his common effectiveness areas or it might be that he has no job at all.

7.1.4 *A Vice President*
A vice president with four subordinates found he had no job.

A Canadian vice president supervised four managers of profit centres as shown in Figure 6. He knew he had difficulty in determining his own specific effectiveness areas. One could not be profit as this was an area of each of his subordinates. He had no resources such as capital to allocate among them and was not responsible for long

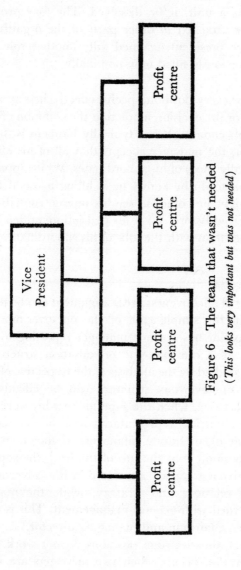

Figure 6 The team that wasn't needed
(This looks very important but was not needed)

run strategy concerning them: in fact, he did not have a job. At a team objectives meeting held for this unit it became clear he had no job. The team recommended that, as a unit, it be dissolved. The four profit centres became attached to other parts of the organisation and the vice president assumed fully another role which he had previously filled only nominally.

Clearly for every position, specific effectiveness areas must be identifiable or the decision made that the common effectiveness areas are job enough. What typically happens is that, on the first attempt, the manager accepts that all of his effectiveness areas are really those of his subordinates. While apparently left with nothing to do he knows he is filling a useful role. With further thought he comes to see his unique contribution only dimly perceived before. With his real job identified he gets on with it rather than with the jobs of his subordinates.

7.1.5 *One-over-one*

The concept of effectiveness areas alignment can be illuminated further from the simple case of the one-over-one situation, where a superior has a single manager reporting to him. The true nature of a one-over-one organisation structure can in fact be best studied by the analysis of the respective effectiveness areas. The one-over-one structure can be effective. It can occur, for instance, when the superior sees his work primarily as that of an 'outside' representative and the manager sees his work as that of an 'inside' manager, as shown in Figure 7. If the top position is at the top of the firm, the superior may have effectiveness areas associated with government and community relations and strategy, while the manager has areas concerned with general management. This is a common split between chairman and managing director.

Sometimes, one-over-one positions do not work because of overlap. Overlap occurs when two managers are responsible for the same thing, so that one of them is not needed.

British industry has in the past suffered seriously from overlap and still does to some extent. We have already seen that at least one British firm discovered, on putting in MBO, that the

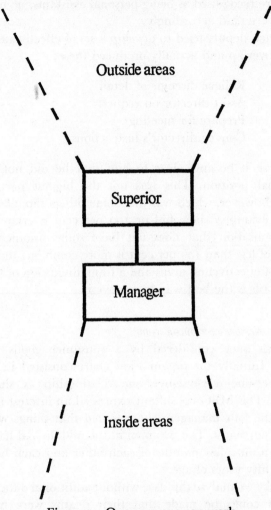

Figure 7   One-over-one can work
(*If one is an outside man and one an inside man,
effectiveness can result*)

effectiveness areas of the directors were identical with those of the deputy directors. The deputy directors, or the directors, if you like, had no job. The clarity with which MBO made this point led to the removal of the deputy positions. There is nothing wrong with having such deputies, of course, as long as they are recognised as being personal assistants, no more, no less, and are paid accordingly.

One such deputy tried to develop a set of effectiveness areas without overlap and actually produced these:

> Relieve director of detail
> Assist director on request
> Prepare for meetings
> Convey director's instructions

With these it became clear to him that he did not have a managerial position. This was not the biggest part of the problem however, which was that some others thought he did.

These examples show full or 100 per cent overlap. It is a rare organisation that does not have some instances of it. Overlap of less than 100 per cent is more common; the identification of effectiveness areas and a frank discussion of them on a team basis is the best way to remove it.

7.1.6 *One-over-one-over-one-over-one*

MBO was once considered by a consumer goods firm in Toronto. Initially the organisation chart consisted in part of a one-over-one-over-one-over-one relationship as shown in Figure 8. The MBO consultant expressed an interest in interviewing the four managers but was told that things were not that way currently. The two men in the middle had had heart attacks within a few months of each other and each had died at under fifty years of age.

It is risky to analyse this case without additional data, but an argument could be made that their deaths were hastened because the two men tried too hard to make an impossible structure work. No job could possibly exist for the two middle men.

Clearly the alignment of effectiveness areas, effectiveness standards and objectives is at the centre of issues concerned with organisation design. These cannot be solved by setting

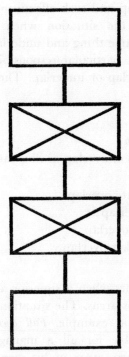

Figure 8 Two men died

(Perhaps an extreme example but the two middle men did have heart attacks at less than fifty years of age)

better objectives. The solution must come from changing the organisation. For these reasons Effective MBO puts great emphasis on change.

While not dealing obviously with the human side of things, this chapter can be used to explain much about human behaviour in organisation. An organisation with well aligned effectiveness areas is a quiet and pleasant place to work in.

7.2 Overlap – Underlap – Alignment

To generalise on the point made in the examples so far, a sound MBO implementation must avoid effectiveness areas

95

overlap and underlap and seek effectiveness areas alignment. Overlap refers to the situation when two positions are responsible for the same thing and underlap when no position has been assigned a particular responsibility. Alignment is a condition of no overlap or underlap. These are illustrated in Figure 9.

7.2.1 *Types of Overlap*
There are four types of overlap as illustrated in Figure 10.

> Duplicate overlap
> Full overlap
> Partial overlap
> Co-worker overlap

Duplicate overlap occurs when a superior and a manager have identical effectiveness areas. The situation of the director and his deputy is a good example. *Full overlap* occurs when a superior is responsible for all a manager does plus some additional effectiveness areas of his own. This might occur with a brand manager reporting to a marketing director who makes all the decisions about brands thus reducing the brand manager to a clerk.

Partial overlap occurs when a superior-manager pair have not fully sorted out their effectiveness areas. In some parts of the job the locus of authority and responsibility is not established. The same kind of thing can occur with co-workers, when it is called *co-worker overlap*.

While the idea of overlap seems so clear as to be almost trite, it nevertheless is still a major cause of low managerial effectiveness and poor implementation of MBO.

The unit effectiveness description helps to clear things up. It is a written statement which specifies the effectiveness areas, effectiveness standards and authority of a unit, its superior and its managers. It separates and then brings together all the elements and so identifies overlap or underlap problems.

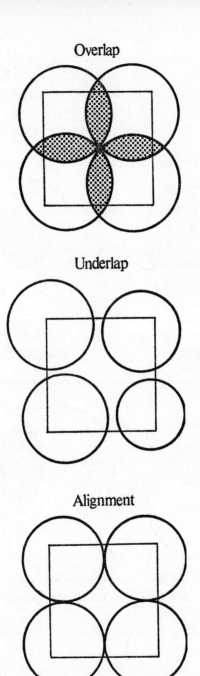

Figure 9   Overlap-underlap-alignment

*(The shaded overlap is duplication, the white space underlap is
unassigned responsibility, alignment is best)*

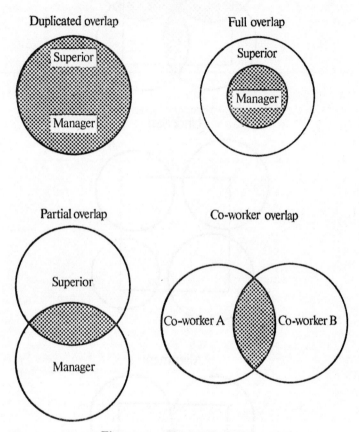

Figure 10 Types of overlap
(*All are expensive and all can be avoided*)

7.3 Alignment and MBO

When one thinks in situational rather than managerial terms the importance of a proper alignment of effectiveness areas, effectiveness standards and objectives becomes obvious. Failure to align provides an important explanation of many unsuccessful attempts to implement MBO. The present position is something like this:

(Alignment of the effectiveness areas and effectiveness standards between levels.)

Can be difficult to do and is usually done poorly. If done well the problems that arise from having a layer of too many managers would be brought out.

(Alignment of the objectives between levels.)

Usually easy to do when an overall plan exists.

(Alignment of the effectiveness areas and effectiveness standards among co-workers at the same level.)

Can be done easily if clear functional area distinctions exist. 'Who has the power?' must often get resolved first.

(Alignment of the objectives among co-workers at the same level.)

Usually fairly easy to do but conflicts arise if roles, power distribution and organisation structure are right but misunderstood or are wrong.

This suggests that effectiveness areas and effectiveness standards are most difficult to align vertically, though when an overall plan exists it is not so difficult to align objectives. Also, effectiveness areas and effectiveness standards can be aligned horizontally but questions of power distribution must often be settled first. The horizontal alignment of objectives may be easy but this too must involve agreement on such things as roles, power and organisation structure.

This emphasis on vertical and horizontal alignment is carried clearly in the definition of Effective MBO:

> 'The establishment of effectiveness areas and effectiveness standards for managerial positions and the periodic conversion of these into measurable time-bounded objectives linked vertically and horizontally and with future planning.'

Get the organisation right then move to objectives.

New concepts introduced – Chapter 7

AREAS ALIGNMENT:
> When effectiveness areas for a set of related positions have no overlap or underlap.

HORIZONTAL ALIGNMENT:
> When the manager's effectiveness areas and objectives mesh well with those of other managers at his level.

MANAGER EFFECTIVENESS AREAS:
> The effectiveness areas of a particular managerial position considered alone; they do not include the effectiveness areas of subordinates.

OVERLAP:
> When two positions are responsible for the same thing. May refer to effectiveness areas or objectives.

UNDERLAP:
> When no position has been assigned the responsibility for a result it is necessary to obtain. May refer to effectiveness areas or objectives.

UNIT EFFECTIVENESS DESCRIPTION:

A written statement specifying the effectiveness areas, effectiveness standards and authority of a unit, its superior and its managers.

VERTICAL ALIGNMENT:

When the manager's effectiveness areas and objectives mesh well with those of other managers above and below him.

part three
OBJECTIVES

8 How to Establish Objectives

Companies with clear objectives and established policies are quiet places in which to work.

Don't let others push their expectations onto you until you know your objectives.

Get your margin, then your philosophy.

After the effectiveness areas and effectiveness standards for a manager's position are established they are converted into objectives. An objective is a highly specific statement about what is to be accomplished for a particular effectiveness standard. A single effectiveness standard usually produces a single objective.

The purpose of this chapter is to show how any effectiveness area or standard can be converted into an objective.

The topics taken up in this chapter are:

> Sound objectives are measurable
> The time element
> The quantity element
> The level of the objective
> Priorities of objectives
> Errors to avoid
> Tests of a sound objective

8.1 Sound objectives are measurable

An objective is useful only if its attainment is measurable. If it is not measurable it is impossible to determine whether the objective has been achieved. 'To increase profits' is an unsatisfactory statement of an objective as it does not say how much or when. A better statement would be 'To increase profits to £200,000 during 1972'. Two essential and measurable elements of an objective are:

> Time (how soon)
> Quantity (how many)

Two other measurable elements which are sometimes included in objectives are:

> Quality (how well)
> Cost (how much)

These last two items are often omitted from the statement of the objective, as they are clearly inferred from the wording or the facts of the situation.

8.2 The time element

Time is one of the easiest elements to include in an objective. It should never be omitted. There are four basic forms which are used in this book.

End Form	EO (end of) JUL (By the end of July)
	EO 1972 (By 31st December, 1972)
Beginning Form	BO (beginning of) JUL (By 1st July)
	BO 1972 (By 1st January, 1972)
During Form	DUR JUL–NOV (From 1st July to 30th November)
	DUR 1972 (From 1st January, 1972 to 31st December, 1972)
Specific Form	ON 16th DEC (On 16th December)
	BY 16th DEC (On or before 16th December)

If the year is not stated it means the current year. The end form is most widely used, as objectives are usually in terms of achieving something by a specific date. It is better to express a date in terms of a month end rather than in terms of the beginning of the next month. 31st August seems a long way from 1st September. A focus on the earlier date tends to avoid procrastination. The specific form tends to be used when a manager's objectives interlock tightly with those of others.

> 'By 16th JUL have a recommendation and sample survey results prepared on which package design should be used for product "Y".'

8.2.1 *The long term*

Objectives are most often set for yearly or quarterly time periods. But the battle does not win the war nor the sale win the customer for ever. Managerial effectiveness is not concerned solely with the present or short run but with the long run as well. Objectives, while set for quarterly or one yearly time periods, must still reflect an understanding of the future. A failure to do this can lead to a variety of problems. A marketing manager who decides to introduce a new brand without looking at brand strategy several years ahead is obviously in error. Also in error is a plan to reduce maintenance expenditure without considering long-term machinery capability. Any public servant knows that it is unwise to start in new directions shortly before an election. The larger the unit the longer-term the objectives usually tend to be. As a very rough guide objectives are most often set for the following time periods:

Corporate	(1 year)	(5 years)	(10 years)
Divisional	(1 year)	(5 years)	
Departmental	(1 year)		
Managerial	(3 months)	(1 year)	

If an objective is set for too short a time period, it may be nothing more than a prediction. In the short term nothing much could be done to change things, anyway. If an objective is set for too long a time period, it may be simply a hope, as too many noncontrollable events could occur in the interim.

8.3 The quantity element

All objectives must be quantified in some way or their achievement cannot be measured. If you cannot measure it forget it. The units most often used are monetary or physical but others are also used:

Monetary units:	'£60,000 sales by EO DEC 1972'
Non monetary units:	'Total of 60 new accounts by EO 1972'
	'Reduction in model change time from 28 days to 25 days by EO 1972'
Proportion:	'Average of 28 per cent share of national market DUR 1973'

8.3.1 *Basis for quantity estimate*
Within every objective, whether explicitly stated or not, one thing, state, condition, or amount is compared with some base. As most objectives aspire to superior performance, implicit in them is some comparison with the past period. An objective which simply states '100 units' is often another way of saying '10 units more than last year'.

Examples of the many possible bases which can be selected for an objective are:

Past period:	x per cent above 1972
Units processed:	x per cent of those handled
Other's forecast:	x per cent of *Marketing Guide*'s market estimate
Competitors:	per cent of market
Market statistics:	per cent of disposable income

Utilisation:	per cent utilisation of space
	per cent utilisation of capital
	per cent utilisation of stock
	per cent utilisation of machinery
Deviations from:	Within a range of . . .
	Not outside of . . .
	With $(+)$ $(-)$ x per cent of . . .

This kind of wording is often used with standard costs, deadlines, forecasts, targets, budgets, and PERT and CPM networks.

8.3.2 *Unsatisfactory quantity indicators*
It is not satisfactory for objectives to use such words as the following without specific quantification:

> Increase
> Decrease
> Maximise
> Minimise
> Satisfy
> Optimise

These words at most indicate direction only and not how much.

8.3.3 *Qualitative objectives not usually necessary*
Most so called 'qualitative' objectives should not be considered objectives at all but should simply be called 'activities'. For any qualitative objectives, 'Why?' should be asked, and then the conversion from input activities to output objectives should be made.

On the left below is a list of qualitative objectives which are used as an illustration in one popular MBO book to suggest that such qualitative objectives must sometimes be used. This is incorrect. To illustrate, on the right are this author's conversions to show that such qualitative objectives are usually unnecessary.

Suggested qualitative objectives in standard MBO book	*Effective MBO conversion to illustrate that qualitative objectives are usually found to be activities. By asking the purpose of the activities the quantitative objectives are derived*
Conduct monthly management development sessions for superintendents in techniques of standard cost programme.	Have 50 per cent of superintendents using standard cost programming techniques on at least two projects by EO JUL 1972.
Prepare a programme for patent protection.	Have no patent loopholes in our patents discovered by our staff, independent agents or competitors DUR 1972.
Prepare and distribute an internal public relations manual.	Obtain an average of 75 per cent unaided recall, by all non-managerial employees, of 50 per cent of the key corporate activities, or accomplishments of the prior month for each month DUR 1973.
Improve statistical reports to reduce time lag between production and publication dates.	Without decreasing usable content reduce by an average of four days the time to distribute the following reports by EO SEP 1972.
Prepare quality control manual for supervisors.	85 per cent of first line supervisors to know eight of the ten key points in company quality control practice by EO DEC 1972.

Improve appearance, packaging and design of products.	For each item in product line, design a package which will receive more consumer jury votes than any competing product by EO NOV 1972.
Undertake to ally research efforts more closely with production needs.	Have at least 80 per cent of proposals to production manager accepted DUR 1972.

It is true that most of these conversions from inputs to outputs involve a broader view of one's job, a greater responsibility for the staff function and a higher cost of measurement.

8.3.4 *Specific, not general*
In addition to having clear time and quantity elements, the thing referred to in the objective must be stated unambiguously; examples are:

General	*Specific*
Staff	Hourly paid staff in factory 'A'
Product Sales	Products 'A' and 'D'
Customers	Class 'B' and 'F' accounts who have made purchases in the past six months

Such specificity facilitates measurement and certainly aids clear thinking about MBO.

8.4 The level of the objective

An objective should be attainable with a manager's level of motivation, competence, and resources, and it must be tied to the corporate plan. The objective must reflect the manager's and his subordinates' level of experience, training, skill, capability and motivation. It must also reflect the level of resources that the manager can obtain. Objectives may well reflect a more ambitious level of performance than previously. This is expected to result not from working harder but from working smarter and with better vertical and horizontal alignment.

The quantitative element of an objective may reflect levels:

> As they have been in the past
> As they are now
> As they could be now
> As they could be in the future

The selection the manager makes will depend on many things. It is one of the most important decisions he will make. He must decide what the appropriate level of effectiveness is for himself. He must decide on whether he has the skill and motivation to improve. He must decide on whether a re-arrangement of his or his subordinates' jobs could lead to levels of achievement previously unobtainable. The decision requires a manager to consider his previous level of attainment. Was it too low? Is there anything he can do about it? To be avoided is the predictive objective which simply sets the level at what could probably be attained without any effort.

Sophisticated MBO implementations lead to a variety of objectives being tied to different budget levels. A marketing manager will say, 'I can obtain 32 per cent of the market if I am given a market budget of £800,000, but with £900,000 I can obtain 35 per cent'. One president says:

> 'Our budgets are not an objective, but are the results of objectives. Each year we operate with a minimum budget level which represents the amount of money we believe it is going to cost to do a job which satisfies our minimum objectives and in which we have a high confidence level. We also operate with a quota level, which represents substantially increased performance. Financial plans are made for both levels of operation and are determined to be possible and practical. Budgets indicate what we expect to spend to get the job done. Within the budget we indicate the most important factors. And these are

the standards which represent the percentage of the sales dollar we are willing to spend to get various parts of the job performed. Obviously, the standards are more important than the budgeted amounts, since we are willing to spend more money than we have budgeted if we can get the increased business on standard costs.'

The factors to consider when deciding on the level of an objective are:

> Level necessary to achieve one to five year plans
> Objectives of associated positions
> Budget available
> Possible additional budget available
> Skill of manpower resource
> Motivation level of manpower resource
> Past performance experience

Some managers like the concept of the 'ratchet principle' sometimes called 'stretch'. Both of these refer to obtaining a higher performance than previously with a similar resource level.

8.5 Priorities of objectives

The importance of each objective should be indicated by assigning it a priority of 1, 2, or 3. Number 1 is assigned to the objective of highest priority, and so on. Several objectives may have the same priority. Such assignment of priorities helps to keep a perspective especially when there are many objectives for one position.

With only a few objectives, it is a relatively simple matter to assign priorities. When there are many objectives assigning relative weight is more difficult. An aid to doing this is the method of paired comparisons. The procedure is as follows:

1 Each objective is assigned a number.
2 The basis for assigning priority is established. This

would presumably be 'its importance to the position' or 'its importance to the company plan'.

3 Each objective is compared with each other objective, and one of them is assigned a higher priority.

4 The number of choices each objective receives is tallied, and from this the objectives are arranged in the order of priority.

5 The rank orders are converted to priorities of 1, 2, and 3.

8.5.1 *How many objectives?*

Managerial effectiveness can seldom be obtained by achieving a single objective, no matter how broadly it is written. Effectiveness is multidimensional. Profit, for instance, may be obtained at the risk of losing customers or by sacrificing human resources. Sales may be obtained only by unduly increasing credit risks. Any manager who sees his effectiveness in simple black-and-white terms may perform well in the short term but may not in the long term. On the other hand, a large number of objectives usually indicates only that the essence of the job has not been understood.

8.6 Errors to avoid

In casting up their objectives managers should be wary of these errors which frequently occur:

> Objectives too high (Overload)
> Objectives too low (Underload)
> Objectives not measurable
> Cost measurement too high
> Too many objectives
> Too complex objectives
> Too long time period
> Too short time period
> Unbalanced emphasis

Most of these are self-explanatory and have been discussed earlier.

While opinions differ, more than ten or so objectives probably indicates a fragmentation of the job rather than seeing it as a whole. Complex objectives tend to be produced as hedges against unsatisfactory performance. Hidden in them are 'ifs' and 'buts'. Except for the top team, objectives need not usually cover more than a year, while less than a three month time period is usually considered too short. Unbalanced emphasis would occur if there were five objectives covering 20 per cent of the effectiveness areas of the position and one objective for the other 80 per cent.

Managers should expect that they and their subordinates will make all these errors at least once or twice in the introductory stages of installing an Effective MBO system.

8.7 Tests of a sound objective

Sound objectives can be easily distinguished from unsound ones by being tested against this list.

TESTS OF OBJECTIVES	
Sound	*Probably unsound*
Measurable (Quantitative)	Non-measurable (Qualitative)
Specific	General
Results (Output) centred	Activity (Input) centred
Realistic and attainable	Minimum or unattainable
Time bounded	Time extended

Many factors in this list overlap somewhat, but, taken together as well as separately, they serve to identify clearly the characteristics of sound objectives that managers would want to establish for their positions. A good objective must be *measurable*, for without this its achievement cannot be established. It should be *specific* rather than general, so that what is being measured is unambiguous. 'Most product lines', is not as good a statement as 'product lines A, C, and S'. It should focus on *results* or *output* rather than *activities* or *input*, that is, on what a manager achieves rather than on what he does. 'Implement budget control' is not as good as 'Have budget control system in full operation'. It should be seen as a *realistic* and *attainable* objective to both the superior and the subordinate rather than as a *minimum* or *unattainable* objective. It should be *time bounded* with clear time limits for completion rather than being time extended.

New concepts introduced – Chapter 8

OVERLOAD:

Levels of objectives set too high to be attainable.

PREDICTIVE OBJECTIVE:

An objective based on a prediction rather than a plan.

PRIORITY:

The relative importance of an objective, indicated by the number 1, 2, or 3.

RATCHET PRINCIPLE:

Setting a slightly higher objective than previously attained.

STRETCH:

The difference between past and planned performance.

UNDERLOAD:

Levels of objectives set so low they would be attained without effort.

9 How to Plan to Meet Objectives

Planning is not an addition to a manager's job.

The only difficulty in planning is how to get managers to do it.

Managers should not do things right but do the right things and planning will help them to discover which things they are.

An objective without a plan is a dream.

This chapter shows how to convert an objective into a plan, a plan into a schedule, and a set of schedules into an activity schedule which every manager using MBO needs. Some will be struck by the simplicity with which the topic is treated. It is simple because what is needed is simple not complex. Sound and lengthy books have been written about planning. The average manager, however, needs only the guides given here – and his own decision to start.

A special emphasis is given to manager planning in Effective MBO. This refers to the production of a step-by-step plan which will lead to the attainment of an objective. Corporate planning is an important part of Effective MBO of course, but then so it is in many systems. It is manager planning which is missing. Managers normally resist the discipline involved in planning to achieve their own objectives. But when they have gone through one or two cycles they see what an important tool it is.

Planning is not an addition to a manager's job. It is a way of managing. Managers who say they have 'no time for planning' are those who have no time to get properly organised. MBO properly applied is nothing more than sound management with an emphasis on planning.

For any objective there must be a plan and a timed schedule.

Objectives without plans are dreams. Plans are a statement, prepared in advance, of what is to be done. A schedule is a plan with timings. Without plans managers muddle through to their objectives, which, if achieved, were almost certainly too low to begin with. A plan identifies what is seen as the best route toward achieving an objective. Planning is a purely intellectual process, and to plan well managers need to sit and think.

Sound advance planning has many benefits: it increases a manager's thinking time and decreases his doing time. In this way brains are substituted for effort. Crisis management is less likely to occur, as most eventualities have been thought out in advance. In-basket material will always be drastically reduced, as key activities have been decided and agreed in advance and managers do not need to be continually reminded of them.

Plans may consist of a few simple sequential steps or they may be considerably more complex. While determining and approving objectives is the joint responsibility of the superior and the manager concerned, plans are the sole responsibility of the manager himself. It is his responsibility alone that his plan leads to the achievement of the objective.

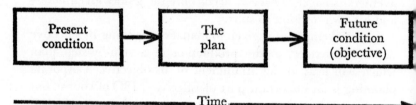

Figure 11　Plans lead to objectives being achieved

(Objectives without plans are dreams; plans convert objectives to reality)

A plan is the means by which it is proposed to convert a present condition to some future condition. The future condition is the objective, as shown in Figure 11.

If the objective could have been achieved without the plan, it was not an objective but a prediction. Managers are not paid simply to allow predicted futures to occur: management is not needed for that. Management is paid to cast up alternative futures, select one of them, which is the objective, and work to achieve it by a plan.

Any plan consists of a series of things to be done called 'activities'.

9.1 What is an activity?

An activity is something a manager does. The key word in the activity should be chosen so that completion of the activity is unambiguous. Such words as *administer, manage, arrange, observe* and others shown in Figure 12 are usually unsuitable

Administer (approve)	Examine (decide)
Analyse (decide)	Expedite (attain)
Arrange (implement)	Facilitate (provide)
Assist (advise)	Follow-up (review)
Assure (notify)	Investigate (decide)
Collaborate (achieve)	Manage (obtain)
Consult (ask)	Observe (appraise)
Cooperate (achieve-inform)	Participate (decide-inform)
Coordinate (decide)	Search (find)
Develop (prepare)	Study (appraise)
Discuss (inform-prepare)	

Figure 12   Poor activity indicators

(The words we use can show we don't mean anything—better but not always appropriate substitutes are in parenthesis)

prefixes for activities, as all have inherently vague meanings and each could mean many different things. Better prefixes are *change, close, complete, decide, deliver, purchase* and *train,* and others shown in Figure 13. While some words such as these can have the defect of ambiguity, they are less ambiguous than the other examples given. The purpose of these two lists is not to initiate a debate on exceptions to the words in them, but simply to make one point clear: the wording of the activity should be such that all involved would know when it is completed. When applicable, *finish* is a better prefix than *start*.

Adopt	Distribute	Provide
Advise	Divide	Purchase
Announce	Draft	Recommend
Appraise	Establish	Record
Approve	Find	Release
Assemble	Formulate	Represent
Assign	Give	Request
Attach	Hire	Require
Authorise	Implement	Requisition
Calculate	Inform	Review
Cancel	Initiate	Revise
Change	Inspect	Schedule
Circulate	Install	Scrutinise
Classify	Instruct	Secure
Collect	Interview	Select
Compile	Issue	Sell
Complete	Locate	Separate
Conduct	Maintain	Start
Control	Make	Submit
Construct	Notify	Summarise
Correct	Obtain	Supply
Decide	Organise	Tabulate
Delegate	Originate	Teach
Deliver	Outline	Tell
Design	Plan	Trace
Determine	Prepare	Train
Discover	Programme	Verify

Figure 13   Better activity indicators

(Most of these words mean that something will get done)

Here are examples of two simple plans, without dates, showing the use of appropriate key words.

Objective:

Increase sales on Product A from 2·6 per cent to at least 2·9 per cent of market during 1971.

Plan (activities):

1 Discover by analysis of sales records of the past four years what are the weak and strong markets and what is the marketing mix impact.

2 Discover competitors' product and marketing mix over the past four years.

3 Conduct a two-day marketing strategy meeting to develop new marketing strategy.

4 Implement the proposed strategy.

Objective:

Increase demands on company computer facilities to 60 per cent utilisation by EO 1971.

Plan (activities):

1 Discover by survey why existing users do not use the service more.

2 Discover by survey why some do not use the service at all.

3 Prepare a draft of my analysis of problem and our proposals on how to increase utilisation and distribute to users and non users.

4 Conduct a one-day meeting to discuss my draft and obtain agreement on improvement methods.

5 Implement the meeting proposals.

9.1.1 *Activity networks*

When the number of activities in a plan goes much over ten, it is often useful to make an activity network. The basic idea is very simple. It involves linking numbers which represent activities with arrows which show the sequential relationship of the activities. A diagram of a particular combination of

Figure 14   A simple network
(*That's not hard, is it?*)

activities and arrows is called an 'arrow diagram' or 'activity network'. The simple network in Figure 14 shows two activities and by the use of the arrow indicates that activity 1 must be completed before activity 2 is started.

A more restricted network in Figure 15 shows that activities 1 and 2 must be completed prior to activity 3, and activity 3 prior to activity 4.

This simple planning concept is of enormous usefulness to managers, and using it can shorten considerably the time taken to achieve objectives. Time is always money. Most managers who do not plan, unwittingly assume that all their activities concerning an objective are sequential. Thus they wait until one activity is completed prior to starting the next. They might instead have initiated work on several activities simultaneously. The reason they do not do this is that they believe their work

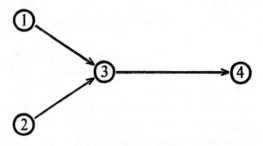

Figure 15   A restricted network

(*Activity 1 and 2 can and should proceed simultaneously and must be completed before starting activity 3—it is simple but is also important*)

may become too complex. They think this because they do not have a plan. Plans simplify and shorten the time to achieve objectives.

Figure 16 shows four examples of networks with five activities having various sequential relationships. Network 1 shows that each activity must be completed in turn before proceeding to the next. In all, five time periods are needed. Network 2 shows that activities 1, 2 and 3 may be worked on at the same time but that all must be completed prior to activity 4, and that activity 4 must be completed before activity 5 is started. Network 3 shows that while activities 1 and 2 may be worked on simultaneously, each respectively must be completed prior to activities 3 and 4 being initiated, and both 3 and 4 must be

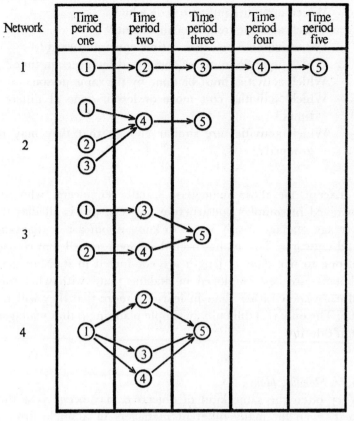

Figure 16 Networks of five activities
(*This kind of analysis leads to things being done faster and on time*)

completed prior to 5 being initiated. Network 4 shows a common type of network for managers. Activity 1 has to be completed and perhaps a plan made, after which several activities may be initiated and completed (activities 2, 3 and 4), usually by a manager's subordinates, and after that a decision or evaluation is made by the manager (activity 5).

In selecting the best activities, and their sequence, the following questions should be asked:

How broad or detailed should the activities be?
Is it best to work backward from the objective or forward to it?

Which activities must precede which?
Which activities may be concurrent?
For which activities does a time constraint exist?
Which activities must be completed by a certain time?
Which activities must be done by the same person?
Which activities cost more or less if done at different times?
Which activities are similar enough that they may be grouped?

Except for those managers, usually engineers, who are involved in complex construction projects, this is all that the average manager really needs to know about arrow diagrams and networks. The art has been developed so well that courses of one to five days in length are conducted in it. Managers, though, are best employed in making plans with what they already know rather than in learning more that they will not use. The only real difficulty in simple planning is that managers don't do it.

9.1.2 *Standing plans*
Very often the same kind of objective may occur year after year, even for many different managers in a single firm. A firm with several brand managers, for instance, will have many objectives concerning brand launch or market penetration. A firm with several plants will have many objectives relating to quality control and other typical production type objectives. It is then often useful to prepare sets of simple carefully worked-out, master standing plans which can be used, at their discretion, by managers who have common objectives.

9.1.3 *Qualities of a good plan*
The tests of a good plan are:

      l Has a clear objective
      l Has clear activity steps

3 Activities are properly arranged in sequence
4 Has suitable progress checkpoints identified

As a manager gains experience with planning, he will grow in his skill to satisfy all these tests with each plan he makes.

9.2 Some plans fail

If a manager's plan does not lead to the attainment of the objective, the plan or its implementation was faulty. At the end of the year, review of the attainment of objectives is most useful, to review the plan of activities itself. Plans fail for one of three reasons: something was left out, something was put in, or the activities of others were not anticipated. As a manager gains experience in planning, partly through some of his plans failing, he will learn how to think more clearly about these three things which arise from poor planning and which lead to failure.

The most common errors in planning are:

Not doing it
Planning only two to four activities when many more are needed
Not recognising that for many objectives several activities may proceed simultaneously
Becoming so fascinated by the plan that its associated objective is seen as secondary
Failure to review a plan when the objective is not met
Omission of key activities
Failure to allow for activities of others that might hinder one's own plan
No review of progress
Stating activities vaguely, so that their completion is uncertain

9.3 Converting plans to schedules

Planning consists of determining the things to be done and the sequence in which they should be done, in order to achieve a given objective. *Scheduling* consists of putting dates on the activities of a plan. As an example:

Objective:
> Have plant in single shift operation at 70 per cent capacity by EO Aug 1970.

Plan:

1	Complete design by	EO Mar 1968
2	Complete construction by	EO Dec 1969
3	Install all equipment by	EO Feb 1970
4	Hire and train staff by	EO May 1970
5	Start-up by	EO June 1970

Planning and scheduling are technically different. Scheduling involves dating the activities of a plan and this is the way scheduling will be referred to here.

9.3.1 *The activity schedule*

If it is assumed that for each of the four networks considered earlier, each activity or set of simultaneous activities took a month to complete, starting 1st January, the timing of each would look like the schedules in the accompanying table.

Plan One	*Plan Two*
1 EO Jan	1 EO Jan
2 EO Feb	2 EO Jan
3 EO Mar	3 EO Jan
4 EO Apr	4 EO Feb
5 EO May	5 EO Mar

Plan Three	*Plan Four*
1 EO Jan	1 EO Jan
2 EO Jan	2 EO Feb
3 EO Feb	3 EO Feb
4 EO Feb	4 EO Feb
5 EO Mar	5 EO Mar

Network	Activities				
	Jan.	Feb.	Mar.	Apr.	May
1	1	2	3	4	5
2	1 2 3	4	5		
3	1 2	3 4	5		
4	1	2 3 4	5		

Figure 17   An activity schedule

(A planning board like this helps a manager keep on target)

These timings can be presented conveniently on an Activity Schedule shown in Figure 17. This schedule shows, for instance, that the manager's plan is to complete seven activities by the end of January, another seven by the end of February, and so on. A trained secretary can assist a manager by giving him a list of activities to be completed for each month in the third week of the prior month, or a wall board may be used. Without having such a schedule a manager cannot be using MBO to plan. With a schedule it will become very clear to him whether he is taking on too big a job or too small; if the job is too big, such a schedule will show what type of assistance is needed, and when.

9.3.2 *Putting dates on plans*
There are some obvious factors which affect the construction of a schedule and some not too obvious. In deciding what dates to put on a plan these factors are most important:

The earliest start point
The latest finish point
Key date ties with other schedules
Staffing required and available for each activity
Equipment required and available for each activity
Uncontrollable timed inputs from others

New concepts introduced – Chapter 9

ACTIVITY:

A particular thing a manager actually does or intends to do.

ACTIVITY NETWORK:

A diagram of a particular combination of activities connected by arrows to show their sequential relationships.

ACTIVITY SCHEDULE:

A visual arrangement of activities over a time period.

PLAN, A:

A sequence of activities.

SCHEDULE:

A plan with timings.

10 How to Measure Performance

Most job outputs are measurable and even St Paul had clear effectiveness areas, though Judgment Day does represent a long performance feedback loop.

Information is at least the lubricant of the business and may be its heart.

To increase their effectiveness, managers should attempt to build situations which have feedback loops incorporated into them. The loop may be simply a candid subordinate who tells the manager quickly when things are not to his liking. The loop would more likely be the measurement of a production process. Effective managers develop short-term feedback loops so that they can get quick readings on the effect of their actions. Psychologists have shown, in a variety of experiments, that performance improves when the results of performance are known. To put it more directly, without feedback there is little learning. To improve our effectiveness, we must have feedback on its effects. Feedback loops are built into many types of technical systems. They are designed to provide corrections to the planned course. Such loops keep guided missiles on target or radio receivers on frequency. When the actual events vary from those planned, they provide a means of correcting the deviations.

A division manager and his seven subordinate managers decided to establish their effectiveness areas and develop their objectives. It was not difficult for these men to see that their performance was measurable, but no data were available for doing it. This led to many changes in accounting and recording procedures, so that ultimately all of them had clearly quantified performance measures on a weekly, monthly, quarterly, or annual basis. Their interest in measurement led directly to a fundamental redesign of part of the total accounting system of the company, which became centred around output measurement rather than input control.

MBO is based, in part, on sound measurement, and unless it exists or can be achieved, MBO can never be a success.

10.1 Are you getting the information you need?

Company information systems vary widely in sophistication, accuracy, usefulness, and timeliness. Few are perfect. Most managers receive information they do not want, and they do not get information they really need. One production manager in a cigarette firm received daily reports on the hours of sun in Kenya but did not receive clear quality control information quickly enough and in the form most useful to him. This kind of thing is common enough almost to be called a natural state. It can be changed, however, if managers, having set clear objectives, insist on being provided with information by which to measure their attainment.

The most important single overall test of any information a manager receives is its usefulness to him. Its usefulness is determined by its relevance to his own objectives, its timeliness, its accuracy and the form of its presentation. If any of these are missing or inadequate the data will be less useful or useless. Many managers complain about the quantity of data they receive or its absence but too few do something about it. It is an easy matter to remove one's name from a distribution list or, failing that, to ask one's secretary to file the report on receipt. Every manager should look closely at the data he himself disseminates and ask himself whether everyone would not be better served with much less of it in a more useful form. Low trust levels is one of the biggest causes of excess paper.

While most managers have a feast of data they do not want, they also have a famine of data they want. This most often arises because they have not asked for it or have not been too clear on what they really want. They do not question established accounting procedures or else they believe them too difficult to change.

10.1.1 *Two kinds of accountants*
There are two kinds of accountants, or other types of information specialists. One is interested in producing immediately useful information; the other, only in keeping records. The primary orientation of each can shape the nature of the information system of the firm. The first type, the effective accountant, is a wonder to behold; he is considered a precious gem, and deserves to be. While wanting to be useful he still has to wait until managers tell him what information they want; more important perhaps is for them to tell him why they want it. Without these statements the willing information expert can do nothing. The second type is usually amenable to change, but not in the short term. He may well have been driven to his position through years of witnessing misused or under-used information. He may even be willing to change immediately but he is naturally suspicious of an overnight change of heart on the part of managers fresh from an MBO course. He does not plan to ask his staff to work months of overtime and to switch his system around just because one director spent a day in London on an MBO course. In most firms, however, some information system redesign is necessary to produce the measurement data required for MBO. The total cost of measurement must be weighed against the use that will be made of the data and the expected benefits of an MBO programme. It is of little value to spend £7,000 on obtaining information which, if properly used, will save less than £1,000.

10.2 Sources of information

Most firms have vast reservoirs of untapped information. Most of it will, thankfully, remain untapped. However, much useful information exists ready made or is easily obtainable, and it is an obligation of the individual manager to do what he can to tap it. The primary sources of data are:

> Central accounting department
> Local accounting departments
> Sales record analysis
> Records check
> Sight checks (visual inspection)
> Internal surveys
> External surveys
> Secondary data

10.2.1 *Central accounting department*

The central accounting department is, of course, a prime source of information, but company accountants are required by law to produce reports in specific forms. They are also required by their profession to follow numerous accounting principles, such as conservatism in valuing assets. The reports so produced are a valuable historical record of a company's progress and are often most helpful in establishing long-term strategy. They are not generally useful, however, as operating guides to the practising manager. These reports are well designed for use outside the firm, not inside it. For instance, why should a manager base his actions on what the Commissioners of the Inland Revenue or the accounting profession think are appropriate depreciation rates? It is a serious error to see performance data for managers based on bits of data collected for other purposes. Progress toward managerial objectives can seldom be measured by a simple one-day slice of the balance sheet or profit and loss account prepared for statutory purposes.

Most of the useful information central accounting departments produce is based on the key figure elements in a cost or profit centre and includes:

> Sales
> Cost of sales

Cost of materials
Cost of production
Cost of distribution
Budget variance
Return on capital

Unless managers are at the top of a profit or cost centre, they may find the information supplied by central accounting departments somewhat too general for them, and so they turn to local accounting departments instead.

10.2.2 *Local accounting departments*
Local accounting departments are likely to provide such information as:

Cost by specific products
Cost by specific markets
Cost of hiring new employees
Scrap level by specific products
Cost of achieving budget objectives

The procedures of local accounting departments are usually locked in fairly tightly with those of the central accounting departments. This makes it difficult to obtain changes locally without changing major parts of the larger system. Supplementary local accounting sub-systems may be introduced, but only at increased cost. Changes may be made locally but should be extensive only when the board has agreed to modify the total system of measurement and reporting – if such a change is needed at all.

10.2.3 *Sales record analysis*
Sales record analysis, or that of any functional area, always has been, and still is, one of the most useful and least used sources of information on such things as:

Order size and trend
Customer types

> Customer distribution
> Impact of the firm's own major marketing strategies
> Impact of competitors' marketing strategies

Many marketing and sales managers could employ clerical help very effectively in mining the information that sales records contain. Most sales managers can recall trends they spotted too late or know what an analysis of the impact of a particular competitor's strategy could provide. After training, medium-grade clerical assistance can provide a wealth of such data at nominal cost. After using such data for a year or so, and after the various snags are ironed out, managers often decide to computerise the sales analysis reporting system. While only sales records have been used for illustration, the general principle of analysis applies equally to production, purchasing, stores, personnel, and other areas.

10.2.4 *Records check*
Probably the most useful but unused information is in the files. It takes but little effort to install a simple counting system to obtain such information as:

> Employee turnover by division
> Damage claims
> Missed delivery dates
> Order errors
> Grievances
> Labour rates

In larger firms, or those with elaborate systems, much or most of this may be generated at the moment. If not, however, it costs little to produce it.

10.2.5 *Sight checks* (visual inspection)
Sight checks are very useful provided the sampling procedure is reasonably fair and unknown in advance to those who might

have reason to want to distort the data. Sight checks might be used for:

> Per cent machine utilisation
> Per cent space utilisation
> System installation

10.2.6 *Internal surveys*
Internal surveys and tests are used to discover such things as:

> Employee attitudes
> Levels at which decisions are made
> Impact of training
> Actual implementation of a system
> Cost of typing a letter
> Reject rates
> Product quality
> Raw material quality
> Reasons for termination

10.2.7 *External surveys*
MBO usually leads to a decision to make some surveys outside the firm. As these surveys can be expensive a serious cost/benefit analysis of the information sought is very important. The type of information most often sought includes:

> Company image
> Product image
> Product display
> Customer satisfaction
> Share of market

The surveys may be made by telephone, mail, personal interview or by inspection. The typical survey respondents include: suppliers, customers, general public, news media, legislators, shareholders, competitors, customers, and many others. It is almost always wise to obtain professional assistance in survey design and analysis. No such survey should ever be initiated unless management can state clearly just what decisions it proposes to make based on the data collected. Such surveys are sometimes conducted to make management feel comfortable; a pillow would be cheaper.

Internal and external surveys are usually expensive. The problem is never measurement but the cost of measurement. If no measurement method exists and if with it performance would increase then clearly some special expenditure is justified.

10.2.8 *Secondary data*
'Secondary data' is information collected by someone else, usually for a general purpose. The best examples are economic trend summaries produced by the banks, trade associations, or the Department of Trade and Industry. Many managers keep informally abreast of such data by reading trade or general business magazines. For special projects or corporate strategy development, however, a special search for secondary data is advisable. Typical of the secondary data available is information on:

> Average work-week manufacturing
> New orders by industry
> Industrial production
> Quarterly gross national product
> Building contracts
> New companies formed
> Industrial share indices
> Retail sales
> Unemployment levels
> Business failures
> Non-agricultural employment
> Personal income
> Quarterly company profits
> Quarterly dividends

10.2.9 *Refinement of measurement*

Even when a measurement method is found it may often be capable of refinement. The right hand members of these pairs illustrate a move toward refinement of measurement:

Gross sales	versus	Contribution to overhead
Per cent increase	versus	Per cent increase adjusted for annual trend
Absolute increase	versus	Per cent increase
Lost time accident frequency	versus	Lost time accidents per 100,000 hours worked

The refined measures are generally better and are less affected by changes over which a manager may not have control. Suppose that one manager had an objective of increasing sales and another that of decreasing distribution cost. If the first were successful it is unlikely that the second would be. This could be corrected easily if instead of 'Decrease distribution cost', 'Decrease distribution cost as a percentage of sales' were substituted.

10.3 Effective data

The usefulness and therefore the effectiveness of the measurement data a manager receives can be assessed by their:

> Relevance
> Timeliness
> Accuracy
> Presentation

The data reaching a manager should be only those on which he can make a decision. If parts of the data do not affect him he should not get those parts. The poorest kind of data are those which enable a manager only to say, 'Old Bill isn't doing too well this month'.

The data must also be available in sufficient time so that appropriate decisions may be made if necessary. If crisis management breaks out whenever the data arrive they should have come sooner or the wrong person is getting them. If no decisions could ever be made on the data, they could probably arrive later or not at all. The data should also come at the right frequency. Some should come daily, others monthly, and so on. Learning experiments by psychologists are virtually consistent in proving that short feedback loops improve performance. If a manager could get immediate feedback on the probable or actual effectiveness of his actions, his performance would improve sharply. The cost of providing these loops must be considered, of course, but so also must their potential benefits. In department stores both senior and junior managers get one-day or shorter-period feedback, and this often occurs in production management as well.

To be useful, data need not be 100 per cent accurate. They need to be only accurate enough so that correct decisions are more likely to be made. To make a report 100 per cent accurate, unnecessarily, incurs a high cost and results in delay. For these reasons sampling techniques of measurement are becoming more and more widely used, though they have already been used for years on such things as market share and product quality.

Managers should decide not only on the data they want and when they should get them, but also on how these data should be presented. Some managers prefer graphs, some tables, and others both. Some want their data cumulative; some look after such records themselves. Some wish to use charts on their office walls, and so on. Any competent senior manager should be willing to support, or at least tolerate, any presentation peccadilloes as long as they help to get the data used.

10.3.1 *The Data Appropriateness Checklist*
For every piece of routine data landing on his desk a manager should complete one column of the Data Appropriateness Checklist shown in Figure 18. After doing so he should initiate the changes required.

	A		B		C	
	Y	N	Y	N	Y	N
DO I WANT IT? (if No, do not answer further questions)						
IS IT RELEVANT TO MY POSITION? (Do I need to have it to make better decisions?)						
DOES IT COME IN TIME?						
DOES IT COME AT THE RIGHT FREQUENCY? (not more or less often than it should)						
IS IT ACCURATE ENOUGH? (not too inaccurate or unnecessarily accurate)						
IS ITS PRESENTATION IN THE BEST FORM FOR ME?						

Figure 18   Data appropriateness checklist

(Complete this for all regularly appearing data crossing your desk)

This checklist asks six questions which relate to the four tests of measurement data.

> Do I want these data?
> Are they relevant to my position?
> Do they come in time?
> Do they come at the right frequency?
> Are they accurate enough?
> Is their presentation in the best form for me?

The use of this checklist and a follow-up on what it reveals usually results in less and better data. The form should be used to cover all written or statistical reports, minutes, carbons of letters, magazines, and virtually anything with an information content appearing in the in-tray. The manager who wishes to be effective will want a major decrease in the bulk of the information he receives. One newly appointed top manager using the form eliminated about 70 per cent of the information reaching him. He said,

> 'I felt quite guilty about it at first but then I realised that I was paying other people to read them and take action on them so why should I?'

10.3.2 *Becoming numerate*

Some managers are literate and some are numerate. Too few are fully numerate, although at the level required in business they could easily be so. A short three-day course could teach all those attending it such things as:

> When statistics lie
> How to sample
> How to calculate breakeven points
> How to predict by extrapolation
> How to use averages
> How to calculate probabilities
> How to read accounting statements
> How to ask the computer the right questions
> How to read charts and tables
> How to smooth complex shapes

A manager who learns to do these simple things, all of which are applied arithmetic, is better equipped to deal with all the data the computer can now, or will, provide.

10.3.3 *Feedback loops design*

The way in which data are supplied to a subordinate is a direct reflection of organisational philosophy and management style. The methods may be categorised as:

> Management by hunch
> Management by tight control

Management by staff
Management by exception
Management by delegation

Management by hunch occurs when there are no feedback loops at all or when there are only a few very long term ones. Management decision making is guesswork at best, and hunch and prejudice are the primary guides to action. An enormous

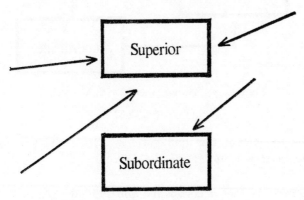

Figure 19   Management by hunch
(*No organised feedback here*)

number of firms operate this way, even those with a large number of reports. The reports they get are not feedback loops on output at all, but duty activity or input reports. Thus management by hunch may be represented as in Figure 19. There is no organised feedback to either the superior or the subordinate.

Management by tight control occurs when information on the subordinate's performance is fed back directly to his superior through a staff unit and then only through his superior to the subordinate. A very large number of information systems are still designed this way. Notice in Figure 20 that the subordinate produces performance data, which are processed by central staff, accounting, or computer staff, who then feed them to the superior, who then passes them to the manager. This design is based on the view that it is management's job to tell subordinates when they make mistakes. The underlying assumption

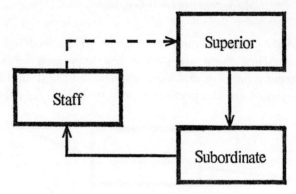

Figure 20   Management by tight control
(*'Now this is how you are doing'*)

appears to be that the manager has neither the wit nor the interest to accept and act on the data himself.

Management by staff occurs when the staff are given, or have assumed, too much responsibility as shown in Figure 21. It may have gone so far that the staff decide the primary

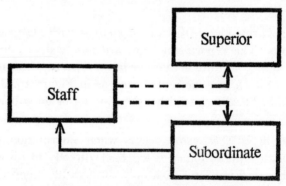

Figure 21   Management by staff
(*'Wait till they read this. Where shall we send it?'*)

measures of managerial effectiveness and, a more serious situation, when it should be released and to whom. There is nothing more de-motivating than having no control over your own performance feedback. This method should always be discouraged. It occurs most often when managers do not see system management as their job and so abdicate their responsibility to the staff.

Management by exception is an acceptable method of managing feedback in large organisations. The manager gets all the data he generates and his superior gets only the out-of-control data as shown in Figure 22. This method is particularly

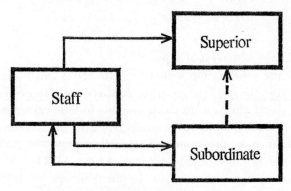

Figure 22   Management by exception
(*Out-of-control data only*)

appropriate if the superior has to co-ordinate several functions. In this case he must know when one function is out of control. It is often possible, however, to remove this co-ordination function from the superior if it does exist. Improved information systems make it possible for managers to co-ordinate themselves.

Management by delegation occurs when a subordinate is given authority and responsibility and he decides what data to feed back to his superior as in Figure 23. This method is what most managers would prefer to work under. It is highly motivating.

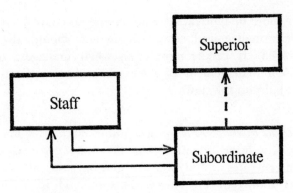

Figure 23   Management by delegation
('*Tell me only what you think I need to know*')

10.3.4 *Major philosophical differences*

Clearly the information system tied to MBO can be installed using any of the last four methods. As there are major differences among them, the four methods amount to four varieties of one aspect of MBO. Individual managers and organisations will have their own preference. This will depend on how they define the organisational problems which MBO is intended to clear up and what their implicit theory of individual motivation happens to be.

New concept introduced – Chapter 10

MEASUREMENT METHOD:
  The way in which the degree of attainment of an objective is determined.

11 The Objective Record Sheet

The best MBO procedures are simple, not exotic.

This chapter will show how to bring together on a single sheet of paper what has been covered so far. The Objective Record Sheet is a simple form on which to record an effectiveness area, the associated objective, the priority of the objective and its measurement method, the programme of activities and the actual performance achieved. The effectiveness standard is not included as it may be inferred directly from the objective. This form has many similarities to other forms used to record objectives. Its main difference is the space given to record the complete programme of activities necessary to achieve the objective.

Each objective is recorded on a separate Objective Record Sheet as shown in Figures 24 to 28. This sheet is both a record of objectives and a useful planning document.

11.1 Contents of objective record sheet

Its main headings are:

> Serials
> Effectiveness area
> Objective
> Priority
> Measurement method
> Programme of activities
> Date
> Completed
> Actual performance
> Manager

Serials:

A number is assigned to each effectiveness area, each objective, and each activity. If the effectiveness area is the third a manager has established for his position, then '3' is inserted. If the associated objective is based on the second effectiveness standard for this effectiveness area, then '3.2' is inserted against it. The activities for this objective are numbered sequentially 3.2.1, 3.2.2, 3.2.3, and so on.

Effectiveness area:

Each effectiveness area is identified by one to four words only. Such directional indicators as 'increase' are omitted. There is no space to record the effectiveness standard separately, as the effectiveness standard is apparent from the objective.

Objective:

Under this heading is inserted a statement of what the manager plans to accomplish, stated as clearly and specifically as possible. There may be more than one objective for a particular effectiveness area, in which case additional Objective Record Sheets are used. There is usually one objective per effectiveness standard.

Priority:

Insert 1 or 2 or 3. 1 indicates highest priority. 3 is the lowest. Several objectives may have the same priority.

Measurement method:

A clear statement of how the attainment of the objective is to be measured. If no measurement method is now available, note the steps being taken to provide one.

Programme of activities:

The specific activities the manager will undertake as steps toward achieving the objective. These are essentially inputs, and care must be taken that they are not seen as substitutes for, or supplementary to, the objectives. This list is designed solely to assist with planning. It is the manager's, not the superior's, responsibility that the programme of activities proposed lead to the attainment of the objectives.

Indicate also the best checkpoint date at which the progress toward the objective is to be formally reviewed. List the checkpoint as a separate activity. A common checkpoint time for all objectives may be decided.

Date:

Date by which the activity is planned to be completed or started.

Completed:

Date by which the activity is actually completed or started.

Actual performance:

A record of the extent to which the objective, not the programme of activities, was actually achieved, as measured by the measurement method established, in the time period set. This is worded in similar fashion to the objective so that comparisons may be made. In addition, it includes a statement of whether the objective was over-achieved, just achieved, or under-achieved. If under-achieved, a clear and accurate explanation of why should be given.

Manager:

The signature of the manager whose objective it is. Signing indicates agreement with the objective and the measurement method.

11.2 Examples

OBJECTIVE RECORD SHEET

ORS

SERIAL			
3	EFFECTIVENESS AREA Paper Products Ltd.		

	OBJECTIVE		PRIORITY
3.2	By EO 1972 have Paper Products Ltd. ready to go into full operation with catalogue printed, inventory in stock with forty paper product lines and administrator appointed.		I

MEASUREMENT METHOD
Existence of company, its catalogue, its inventory and its administrator.

	PROGRAMME OF ACTIVITIES	DATE		COMPLETED
3.2.1	Initiate name search UK–EIRE—EEC—EFTA	EO	FEB 72	
3.2.2	Establish product line	EO	MAR 72	
3.2.3	Plan budget	EO	MAR 72	
3.2.4	Appoint Administrator and agree Effectiveness Areas	EO	APR 72	
3.2.5	Contract all test designs and production responsibility	EO	APR 72	
3.2.6	Incorporate	EO	APR 72	
3.2.7	Checkpoint	DUR	MAY 72	
3.2.8	Survey competitors and customers	EO	JUN 72	
3.2.9	Approve all product designs	EO	SEP 72	
3.2.10	Decide staffing and location	EO	OCT 72	
3.2.11	Design catalogue and pricing	EO	OCT 72	
3.2.12	Mail preliminary promotion piece	EO	NOV 72	
3.2.13	Catalogue mailing ready	EO	DEC 72	
3.2.14	Inventory ready	EO	DEC 72	

ACTUAL PERFORMANCE

Figure 24   Paper Products Ltd.

(From nothing to something in fourteen steps)

OBJECTIVE RECORD SHEET

ORS

SERIALS

6	**EFFECTIVENESS AREA** Consumer Surveys

6.2	**OBJECTIVE** **PRIORITY**

OBJECTIVE
Have full report of national consumer survey
(n-2000) available to management EO JAN 71
showing profiles of our ten major products
and the profiles of the main competitors
for each.

PRIORITY 2

MEASUREMENT METHOD
Availability of twenty copies of report to
management and their acceptance of its
quality.

	PROGRAMME OF ACTIVITIES		DATE		COMPLETED
6.2.1	Make final revisions objectives	EO	MAY	71	
6.2.2	Decide question and answer				
	sheet formats	EO	MAY	71	
6.2.3	Select sample	EO	MAY	71	
6.2.4	Proof and print questionnaire	EO	JUL	71	
6.2.5	Mail sample	EO	JUL	71	
6.2.6	Contract for computer and				
	programmer time	EO	JUL	71	
6.2.7	Design analysis procedure	EO	JUL	71	
6.2.8	Complete analysis	EO	OCT	71	
6.2.9	Draft final report of research				
	design and findings	EO	NOV	71	
6.2.10	Write final report and submit	EO	DEC	71	
6.2.11	Reproduce final report	EO	DEC	71	

ACTUAL PERFORMANCE

Figure 25   Consumer surveys

(*It may be staff but it is output*)

OBJECTIVE RECORD SHEET

ORS

SERIALS

| 4 |
| 4.2 |

EFFECTIVENESS AREA Accounting Information

OBJECTIVE   PRIORITY
Introduce new code of accounts fully into all
branches by EO JUL 1971.   2

MEASUREMENT METHOD
All branch accounts coded using new systems
with less than 3 errors in 1,000 discovered by
monthly audit team.

SERIAL	PROGRAMME OF ACTIVITIES	DATE	COMPLETED
4.2.1	Obtain approval to introduce	EO MAY 70	APR
4.2.2	Design implementation plan	EO JUL 70	JUNE
4.2.3	Visit all branches to explain implementation plan	EO AUG 70	SEP
4.2.4	Conduct minimum 3 days training for all account clerks	EO SEP 70	SEP
4.2.5	Introduce in West Branch	EO NOV 70	NOV
4.2.6	Conduct 1 day seminar on West Branch introduction problem	EO JAN 71	JAN
4.2.7	Checkpoint	DUR FEB 71	FEB
4.2.8	Introduce into all branches	EO MAR 71	APR

ACTUAL PERFORMANCE
Introduced new codes of accounts fully into
5 of 6 branches by EO July 1971. East
Branch alone exceeded allowable 3/1000
error rate with 15/1000 error rate in August
inspection. No problems anticipated in
reducing this to desired level. Objective was
substantially achieved.

Figure 26   Accounting information

(*A simple plan but important for those who must adjust to it*)

SERIALS

2	EFFECTIVENESS AREA Subordinate Effectiveness			

2.1	OBJECTIVE All subordinates to have their objectives approved for 1972 by EO Oct. 71 and these objectives to have been tested successfully for horizontal and vertical integration.	PRIORITY 1

MEASUREMENT METHOD
Existence of objectives agreed to by myself, each subordinate, my superior and relevant coworkers.

SERIAL	PROGRAMME OF ACTIVITIES	DATE			COMPLETED
2.1.1	Meeting with team to revise effectiveness areas if necessary	EO	MAY	70	
2.1.2	Meeting with my superior to obtain relevant parts of 1972 corporate plan	EO	MAY	70	
2.1.3	Meeting with team to study corporate plan, and agree on unit effectiveness areas	EO	MAY	70	
2.1.4	Team Objectives Meeting to draft unit and position objectives	EO	JUN	70	
2.1.5	Managerial Objectives Meeting with each subordinate to agree on his effectiveness areas, objectives and measurement methods for 1972	EO	SEP	70	
2.1.6	Meeting with my superior and coworkers as necessary to obtain agreement to unit objectives	EO	OCT	71	

ACTUAL PERFORMANCE

Figure 27   Approval of subordinate effectiveness

(*Do this every year*)

ORS

SERIALS

2	EFFECTIVENESS AREA Subordinate Effectiveness

2.2	OBJECTIVE PRIORITY All subordinates achieve their 1971 objectives. I

MEASUREMENT METHOD
Agreement by myself and each subordinate that
each objective was fully achieved using the
measurement method decided.

SERIALS	PROGRAMME OF ACTIVITIES	DATE	COMPLETED
2.2.1	Hold monthly meetings with AJM and TST to coach on method of achieving their objectives.	DUR 71	
2.2.2	Hold meetings on 12 Feb., 26 May, 4 Jul., and 3 Sep., with team to discuss best method of facilitating the the achievement of the objectives for 1971.	ON FEB 16 ON MAY 26 ON JUL 4 ON SEP 3	
2.2.3	Obtain 25% increase in clerical assistance available to unit during year.	EO JAN	
2.2.4	Be available to any subordinate for a 30 minutes meeting with no more than a four day delay.	DUR 71	
2.2.5	Meet twice, in Jan. and May, with all the superiors of all those managers with whose objectives my subordinates' objectives must align.	DUR JAN 71 DUR MAY 71	

ACTUAL PERFORMANCE
Not fully achieved. Four subordinates
substantially achieved their objectives but
two did not. Reasons: Subordinate JKR was
not coached sufficiently in planning,
subordinate RTI possible difficulties with
production division were not sorted out early
in the year and got worse.

Figure 28   Achievement of subordinate objectives
(*The difficult one with many possible different plans*)

11.2.1 *ORS – New company into operation*

Figure 24 shows one of the Objective Record Sheets of an executive director of a pulp and paper producer. One of his effectiveness areas concerned a new company, Paper Products Ltd., that he was responsible for bringing into full operation. The objective might have been improved by adding a quality measure in terms of sales potential or a favourable comparison between the products of Paper Products Ltd. and those of competitors. The measurement method is clear, again except for the quality measure, though it is still quite satisfactory.

The fourteen-step plan could easily be contracted or expanded in detail, but this is not important. Some managers prefer to work with a few and some with many steps. This manager has used the EO (End Of) date form, except for 3.2.7, the checkpoint.

11.2.2 *ORS – Consumer market research*

Figure 25 is that of a market research project leader. His effectiveness area is one of several he had, including industrial surveys and internal company surveys. The objective is quite well worded, as is the measurement method.

11.2.3 *ORS – New code of accounts*

The measurement method of Figure 26 has a clear quality control measure. The programme provides for planning, a trial run, a checkpoint, and then full implementation.

Note the wording of the actual performance section, which parallels that of the objective and states deviance clearly. No explanation was given, but might have been, of why the objective was not fully achieved.

11.2.4 *ORS – Setting objectives with subordinates*

Figure 27 shows a plan to meet an objective associated with a common effectiveness area. It is highly advisable to make even simple plans like this. When not made, the associated activities tend to be delayed unduly, and personnel associated with the achievement have difficulty in making plans of their own.

11.2.5 ORS – *Subordinates meeting objectives*

A second objective associated with the subordinates' effectiveness area is that concerning meeting objectives set. Figure 28 shows such a plan. This plan involves, in essence, a high degree of coaching assistance, especially for two subordinates. Such a plan as this commits a manager's time and enables everyone concerned to mark diary dates.

The mechanics of MBO have thus been covered; we now turn to implementation.

New concept introduced – Chapter 11

OBJECTIVE RECORD SHEET (ORS):

A form used to record a single objective of one effectiveness area and the priority, measurement methods and associated activities of that objective.

part four

IMPLEMENTATION

12 Elements of Successful MBO

For a truly effective MBO implementation the firm must first be made more flexible.

Resistance to MBO introduction or any other change is best seen as rational and logical and the best method to overcome it is by reason.

Poorly implemented MBO can freeze a poor organisational design so things will never improve.

A main design problem in MBO now is in producing a sound second generation implementation procedure for firms where it failed the first time.

MBO implementation has obviously failed if managers are not committed to their objectives.

MBO clearly has great potential for improving effectiveness. However, it must be very carefully implemented or things may well end up worse than before.

12.1 The dark side of the moon

A strength and weakness of MBO is that it appears to be so obvious and simple to introduce. While there have been many successful implementations, by far the majority of attempts end in what must be called failure. Many firms in the United States, United Kingdom and Canada claim to be using MBO when insiders could tell another story.

MBO projects are sometimes formally abandoned: Wickens reports:

> A number of the earlier British applications failed, however, in the sense that management by objectives did not become institutionalised. In one large company, the method was introduced successively in three units between 1961 and 1964. The units were in the heavy electrical, electronics and heavy mechanical industries, situated at widely separate locations. In each case, some benefits were obtained, but the programme was discontinued after a year or two.

A senior consultant in one large consultancy firm recently was asked how many years his firm had spent on MBO implementation. He replied, 'last year, none, but we spent about five man years on taking it out'. This view is perhaps a bit unusual but any wise manager would at least note it.

Tosi obtained some illuminating quotes about MBO by managers exposed to it:

> I haven't had to answer to my boss for the fact that I haven't set objectives yet this year. We need some indication that management is really behind us. I can't really be sure.

> I could not guess what would happen if goals were missed. I don't know anyone who has ever obtained any 'negative' feedback. I don't believe everyone in the company met all their goals. What good is it if we don't know how well we did?

> . . . everyone was interested in this a year ago. This year, it just fell between the chairs. No one picked it up, except personnel. My boss never asked me about it, I haven't set my objectives yet.

Comments from selected samples must always be suspected. However, these do demonstrate that things can go wrong or are seen to go wrong.

12.1.1 *Why MBO sometimes fails*

Some of the reasons causing MBO to fail are said to be:

> Lack of commitment
> Top managers not involved
> Poor implementation methods
> Little coaching and assistance
> No follow-up
> Objectives handed to subordinates
> Creative goals stifled
> Fuzzy top policy
> Overemphasising appraisal
> Making it mechanical

The rest of this chapter, and this book, outlines an implementation method which can avoid these problems. Much has been learned about MBO in the past ten years. What is now clear is what can go wrong, and why. Most important, however, we know how to avoid failure – and this is the topic of this chapter.

12.2 The elements of success

A successful MBO implementation obviously depends on a lot of things. It is becoming clearer, however, that the most important is human involvement. Without commitment MBO can never really be a success. How can commitment be obtained?

The emphasis in Effective MBO, much of which is shared by other MBO approaches, is as follows:

> Adequate unfreezing
> Emphasis on change
> Acceptance of the human side
> Maximum information
> Group emphasis
> Effectiveness emphasis

> Situational emphasis
> Proper entry point
> Appropriate rate of change
> Instrumentation

These ten elements lead to commitment and involvement, the only basis of a well working MBO system.

12.2.1 *Adequate unfreezing*

'Unfreezing' is the single item missing most often from current MBO implementations. The idea behind unfreezing is that if you want to change something you must first loosen it up. MBO is a powerful change catalyst but it needs some behavioural assistance to induce flexibility into an organisation – to prepare a way for the arrival of many proposals for change which MBO inevitably brings. Without unfreezing, managers at most accommodate to MBO – they do not engage it. An almost classical error in MBO is to use it to freeze a poor structure. The organisation wants MBO only as long as nothing really changes. Since an emphasis on outputs and effectiveness usually brings change, the kind of MBO which freezes is usually based on inputs.

Organisations typically need to loosen up a little before they start to change. Many organisations have become frozen around their technology or their past and do not have resources to commit to any major change. The unfreezing process can be provided by the proper introduction of MBO. The key parts include all the things mentioned in this chapter but in particular:

> Acceptance that present conditions are unsatisfactory
> Acceptance that something new is needed to move the organisation ahead
> Time involvement of the top team in a programme of change
> A clear idea of the ideal future state
> A clear idea of the benefits the ideal state will bring

A large number of managers involved

A comprehensive well planned programme to facilitate the change

Early success experiences in moving from the prior state to the new

These conditions cannot be created by a memo or an ordinary meeting, no matter how complete. They can be created by the methods outlined in the remaining chapters.

12.2.2 *Emphasis on change*

MBO is sometimes mistakenly used only to pin things down and not to loosen things up. Clearly MBO provides clarity as to the true functions of an organisation's sub-parts, but it must also create conditions of change for these sub-parts. When MBO is put in by those who think they are writing conventional job descriptions the organisation can become dull rather than lively.

MBO may be seen as a type of management system which can be implemented independently of other systems. Alternatively, it can be seen as a comprehensive framework within which to change an organisation in fundamental ways. It is a fact that when well implemented, MBO leads to major changes.

For this reason it is becoming customary to see MBO as an organisational-change device rather than simply as a management development, planning, or measurement scheme. MBO, in fact, is used as a vehicle to achieve other broad objectives which at first glance are remote from it. These include unfreezing the organisation, mangement revitalisation, team building, developing a marketing orientation, introducing participative management, decentralisation, colonising a new structure, and emphasising the human side of mergers.

MBO often leads to structural changes. Such changes are not always predictable in advance but it is desirable if they can be. Such changes should arise solely from an attempt to design a structure which reflects the objectives of the organisation.

MBO implementation is a problem because MBO is so

powerful that it must lead directly to change to be truly successful. MBO is a good tool to identify waste and inefficiency, and unless a method exists to remove this waste and inefficiency, then MBO cannot properly be implemented. MBO demands organisational and managerial flexibility and a low resistance to change. Unless these conditions exist initially, or are created, then MBO is difficult to implement.

Because MBO is clearly a change catalyst, its very power, if not used properly, generates problems. For MBO to be implemented successfully, a climate for change must be present or must be created. To do this, the firm should have an interest in and an understanding of effectiveness. It is in the name of effectiveness that any changes are being made. In addition, a high trust level must be present. Nights of the long knives are quick ways to change things but most expensive in the long run.

12.2.3 *Acceptance of the human side*

The greatest single factor in any change is the human factor. Important are such things as personal value systems, informal relations, personal ambitions, preferred career routes, and intellectual and emotional capacity. Some of these may be seen as emotional or even irrational factors to consider, but they are as real and as important as any other.

Some managers deride the human factor in change. They fear that they might be seen as soft or that human considerations might interfere with those of managerial effectiveness. This is an inappropriate point of view, as any change inevitably has human consequences which, if ignored, can lead to disaster.

Lack of recognition of the human side of change can waste money, time, and people. A manager moved to desertion through mismanaged change is as much to be pitied as blamed. The money cost of his withdrawal from involvement can sometimes be estimated, and it is high. The personal cost to him, in anxiety and then in loss of personal satisfaction in his work, is incalculable. The negative influence he has on his subordinates must also be considered as a major cost.

Production organisations are basically social institutions.

Technological change almost inevitably leads to social change. Social resistance almost inevitably leads to lower productivity than planned. Managers need to see their job in socio-technical terms. They must see work and relationships as inextricably bound together. To change one, we must understand and manage both.

One of the early but often unstated questions in any change is, 'How will this affect me?' An understanding of how a change might be seen by those concerned with it is clearly essential to effective change introduction. Any experienced manager can recall many examples of resistance to change directly from his own experience. The resistance may have led to a drop in accuracy, productivity, profits, or morale. To some extent the resistance was anticipated, but it may have become more extreme and persistent than was expected.

Sometimes resistance to a particular change is clear to all concerned in such a statement as, 'Sure, his style changed. He used to be an autocrat; now he is a hypocrite.' Or, from a farmer, in reply to advice from an agricultural expert, 'I ain't farming now as well as I know how.' Or, 'That's the best method I have seen, but it is not my way.'

More often it is covert and takes one of these forms:

> 'This is a step backward.'
> 'This is being done too quickly.'
> 'This is not necessary.'
> 'This has not been thought out.'
> 'They have something against us.'
> 'It is being shoved down our throats.'
> 'No one asked my opinion.'

Although some of these points in a particular situation may have validity, they still reflect resistance to change. Resistance to change occurs at all levels in an organisation. It is just as likely to occur at the top as at the bottom.

All managers should ask themselves 'when I resist change do I usually have what I believe are sound reasons for doing so?' Most will say yes. They should then ask 'when others resist change I introduce, do I understand the sound reasons they have for doing so?' Most will say no. A skill managers need to acquire is the ability to understand the real reasons why change is resisted.

Very often, those who resist change become less articulate in expressing their true reasons for resisting it. They are anxious and do not believe they will be heard out in any case. An effective manager therefore must be good at analysing the reasons himself or good at creating conditions of trust so people will tell him what is on their mind.

12.2.4 *Maximum information*
When involved in any change, management goes through four distinct steps:

1 Recognises change needed
2 Decides on ideal state
3 Designs method of implementation
4 Implements change

These should in turn lead to four appropriate announcements:

1 That a change will be made
2 What the decision is and why it was made
3 How the decision will be implemented
4 How the decision implementation is progressing

Each announcement can produce a particular resistance:

1 To the thought of any change
2 To the decision itself
3 To the method of implementation
4 To the changed state itself

When analysing a change in process or when planning a change, these twelve elements should each be considered in turn. In particular, management should consider how well it is conveying the four separate elements of information required. There is a tremendous fear of incomplete information, and people usually fear the worst.

The first piece of appropriate information – that a change will be made – is often omitted or left to rumour; the second – what the decision is and why it was made – is often made too tersely; the third – how the decision will be implemented – is often omitted and not enough thought, let alone communication, given to it; the fourth – how the decision implementation is progressing – is seldom communicated, particularly when there is little that is good to communicate.

Maximum information is usually a sound policy after a change has been announced and sometimes, but not always, before it is announced. Testing the wind with hints about forthcoming changes can sometimes provide useful pointers on the state of resistance to or acceptance for the change. On the other hand, it can simply raise the level of anxiety and lead to wild rumours. Prior announcements should be crystal clear as far as they go, but they do not have to be complete.

A vague sort of prior announcement or rumour is harmful: 'MBO is going to be used.' Rather, a precise prior announcement is helpful:

> 'MBO will be introduced in the top two levels of our A division starting on 1st September. The implementation will be carried out during the following two months. Each manager will participate in a team objectives meeting and a managerial objectives meeting. The pre-work and design of these sessions are available from Mr. Jack Daniels to anyone who wishes to see them.'

Once a change has been announced, the maximum possible information should be distributed about it. Resistance to change is almost always lower if the objectives, nature, methods, benefits, and drawbacks of the change are made clear to all concerned.

Face-to-face announcements are better than the printed word. Not only do they personalise what may be seen as a depersonalised action, but they also allow anxieties to be expressed clearly and perhaps dealt with on the spot.

12.2.5 *Group emphasis*

Management training is now moving more and more to a group or team emphasis. It is becoming clear that the individual group member in isolation can have little influence without the wholehearted co-operation of the others. The best way to obtain this co-operation is to train the managers as a team so that all ideas are team ideas which the team is committed to as a unit.

Unlike some other MBO systems, Effective MBO places great emphasis on teamwork. This approach is fully explained in Chapter 14. During the implementation of Effective MBO the highest proportion of the time spent in discussing effectiveness areas, effectiveness standards and objectives is with the full team, not, as is most common, only between the superior-subordinate pair. Effective MBO must be, and is, a co-operative enterprise. It needs to involve co-workers just as much as it needs to involve hierarchy. Before a team is going to set sound effectiveness areas, effectiveness standards and objectives, it must be given an opportunity to discuss the team and how it is put together and how well or how poorly it works. Changes are then always made and always need to be made. Without the self diagnosis first and unless such changes are made, effectiveness areas, effectivenesss standards and objectives become a patch-up job to satisfy existing conditions rather than to change them.

This method of group emphasis involves participation. The word *participation* itself has not been used, however, as there is so much misunderstanding about, and disagreement over, what it means. 'Participation' need not imply that management will accept all the ideas suggested. Participation can be used quite successfully when management says, in effect, 'This much is decided. What are your thoughts on the rest? We will consider all your proposals but cannot guarantee to accept them.'

The success of methods involving participation depends on the extent to which they are seen as legitimate, honest, and likely to be successful. Although it can be done, it is difficult for a company to start too suddenly to use participation in situations where it has never been used before. A certain degree of trust is important; a certain degree of skill in implementation is crucial; some form of unfreezing is useful. Needless to say, a manager cannot use these techniques if he has already finally settled on a course of action. To do so is both dishonest and foolish. 'You can fool some of the people . . .' and it only takes one to tell the rest. Pseudo-participation is time wasted for everyone and clearly inappropriate if a degree of meaningful participation could have been used instead.

12.2.6 *Effectiveness emphasis*

Effective MBO has clearly stated its position with its name. Effectiveness is the core of a manager's job, as it must be with a management system such as MBO. This emphasis on effectiveness starts with the close attention given to effectiveness areas and effectiveness standards. The major part of this book deals with these concepts. If a manager gets these incorrect, there is little point in going on to set objectives. Once effectiveness areas and effectiveness standards are identified correctly however, objective setting becomes obvious. Many MBO systems still allow objectives to be based on managerial inputs rather than on outputs and many examples are given in Chapter 6. Effective MBO goes so far as to say that if a job cannot be expressed in output terms the job is not needed; also, that these outputs should be 100 per cent of the position. The emphasis on effectiveness is further driven home with the sharp distinction made between managerial effectiveness, apparent effectiveness, and personal effectiveness.

12.2.7 *Situational emphasis*

Too many MBO systems see a manager simply as an entity with a superior above him, but organisation life is much more complex than that. Any manager's position is intimately linked with many other positions and with the organisation and the technology it employs. The relationship may be represented by the diagram in Figure 29.

Most managers have a superior, more than one subordinate and several co-workers. These terms are used in the generally accepted sense. The effectiveness areas of these must be

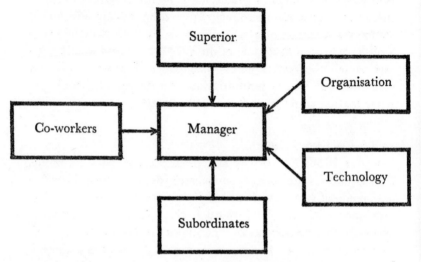

Figure 29   The situation a manager is in

(*A manager is part of a network of relationships with others and with the technology and organisation*)

properly linked or the company can never achieve full effectiveness. 'Organisation', which is short for 'organisation philosophy', is used to refer to all those behaviour-influencing factors which are common to essentially unrelated positions within a social system. This is sometimes referred to as 'extrinsic job factors', 'culture', 'climate', 'values', or simply 'the way we do things around here'. This element is most important in shaping the nature of MBO in a particular firm. MBO to a degree must fit the firm's particular characteristics. Also important, though, MBO must act to change the firm. If it does not do this, the MBO programme is wasted.

'Technology' refers to the way work may be done to achieve

managerial effectiveness. Making widgets, making decisions, and making inspections are forms of work that could be done in ways different from each other; their technology is different. The element is described in detail in Chapter 8, particularly to show the impact of technology on the nature of the best linkage of effectiveness areas, effectiveness standards and objectives across levels.

Each of these makes demands on the manager's style. Clearly a system such as MBO must recognise the demands of all these elements and preferably have an effective method of inducing change in them if change is needed.

12.2.8 *Proper entry points*
In theory there are four possible start-up entry points though in practice only one exists. In theory the entry points are:

> Top team
> Middle management
> Pilot division
> Supervisory level

Top team. The top team does not have to be the managing director and directors, of course. It could as easily be a divisional manager and his subordinates. Whether to start MBO at divisional level depends on the degree of autonomy of the division. Being a profit centre is not enough. The level must have a relatively independent information, policy, procedural and personnel system as well. There is little doubt that the top is the best place to start. Consulting firms that are interested first in quality will accept an assignment only under these conditions. However, MBO must go in properly at the top. One MBO adviser said: 'Our MBO went in at the top all right but it was only for show. Who really made decisions there was never worked out. Each director finished up with about ten sheets of paper describing his job, but they meant nothing.' If one is not rigorous about the top, the benefit of the remaining MBO implementation would be cut by at least 50 per cent.

Another incorrect way of starting at the top, which flies in the face of all we know about motivation, was described as a good method in one MBO book:

'The president's new approach is sketchily outlined here:

> He developed and communicated throughout the company a thoroughly understandable statement of his basic beliefs concerning such matters as free enterprise, the dignity of the individual, the honourable and essential role of profit, and the need for an uncompromising stand on integrity. All management personnel were reminded of the fact that management is the development of people, not the direction of things. Without people, as the president pointed out, the best facilities in the world are meaningless. They were encouraged to understand and help meet the basic needs of all employees, determining the personal objectives of their subordinates and relating these oal s to both departmental and company objectives.

'Constantly the president reiterated:

1 The only reason for being on a payroll is to produce results.

2 The total resources of a business are men, money, materials, time, and space; and their use can be justified only on the basis of positive results.'

This philosophy, which puts both people and results first, is confusing, and in any case, what General Patton might do before a battle is hardly a suitable way to introduce MBO in a modern business organisation. 'At the top' does not mean the top telling others how to do it.

The strength of MBO is that it does not need charisma to make it work, and it certainly does not need the negative and confusing assumptions in that president's mind about motivation. If a top man really believed MBO was any good he would not have to thrust it home with a suddenly discovered philosophy.

Middle management. Starting with the middle management group is acceptable at times. The necessary conditions are that the top start be guaranteed, be not more than six months away, and has been delayed for good reason. It may be, for instance, that the top knows MBO very well and wants the same level of knowledge to be shared more deeply in the organisation prior to a formal start-up.

Pilot division. A pilot division is usable only if it is representative and if the study continues for only up to six months, at which time a report is submitted and a decision is made. Pilots are for testing not delaying. As a poor example:

> One MBO pilot study in a very large organisation was conducted for eighteen months in a part deliberately selected so as not to resemble the organisation but to resemble a business firm instead. A total of four full time staff 'put in' MBO for only eighty managers.

This is clearly not a pilot, but rather a completely un-representative approach.

Supervisory level. MBO should never be first introduced at the supervisory level. If the introduction goes well and MBO is implemented at that level, a tremendous amount of conflict and dissatisfaction will occur.

> One consulting firm, with much skill in MBO, accepted an assignment to put in MBO at the foreman level. It was installed and the consultants and foremen were pleased with it. In a very short time, however, middle and top management were seriously inconvenienced, as the foremen were attempting to manage under a different system from the one that management were accustomed to using.

12.2.9 *Appropriate rate of change*
A common failure in MBO implementations is an attempt to do too much too soon. Top management takes a year or two

in making up its mind and then gives others a couple of months to get on with it. A full-time team is organised, and the rush is on. Very few social systems remain unchanged over long periods. Changes may be small and may be introduced slowly, but they do take place. The discussion of change, therefore, should be concerned not solely with the introduction of change itself, but also with the rate of change.

In deciding on the rate of change, the following factors should be considered:

> Is time important?
> What will be gained by speed?
> What is past custom?
> Will speed increase resistance?
> Can acceptance be sacrificed for speed?
> How would speed be interpreted?
> Are other changes still being assimilated?
> Must other changes be integrated?

There are some general arguments for both slow and rapid change. The arguments for slow change are:

> Usually produces less resistance
> Allows for gradual acceptance
> Will be seen as evolutionary
> Allows for greater understanding
> Allows for skill acquisition
> Changes can blend with others
> Changes, and modifications in the proposed
> change itself, will be easier
> Changes and adjustments to the method
> used will be easier

The arguments for rapid change are:

> Less time taken to reach ideal changed state
> Shorter adjustment period

Only one basic adjustment required
Less basic-plan modification likely
Adds impression of resilience

The speed of change is an important part of any complete plan for reducing resistance. It should be considered carefully along with the methods to be used.

Many managers reading this chapter will have identified the errors they have seen top management make. They might now consider which of the errors they themselves are making with respect to their own subordinates.

12.2.10 *Instrumentation*

One of the most important differences between the implementation method used by Effective MBO and that used by other approaches is the degree of instrumentation used. Training instrumentation generally refers to a training technique which is essentially a meeting in which the specialist in attendance makes only a minor contribution. Such instrumentation is fundamental to most programmed learning approaches. Instrumentation has now developed to a point where it may be used in programmes of change as well as those designed to teach facts. Effective MBO has four such units listed in Figure 30 which are instrumented to a high degree so that large scale in-company application is feasible. The four courses each deal with a different organisational unit – the manager, the managerial team, the superior-manager pair and the top team, be it the board or the executive committee. Together they are designed to bring about the key elements of MBO discussed in this chapter.

The names of the four courses are:

> Managerial objectives seminar (manager)
> Team objectives meeting (team)
> Managerial objectives meeting (Superior-manager pair)
> Corporate objectives meeting (top team)

The managerial objectives seminar is attended by all managers with this book as mandatory pre-reading. At the end of the seminar the concept of effectiveness is clearly understood and every manager has had his effectiveness and effectiveness areas under intense scrutiny. The seminar is described in additional detail in Chapter 13.

Programme	Designed to improve	Who attends	Length
Managerial Objectives Seminar	Managerial Effectiveness	All managers once in stranger teams	3–5 days
Team Objectives Meeting	Team Effectiveness Decision Making and Objectives	All managers twice in work teams, once as subordinate then as superior	3 days
Managerial Objectives Meeting	Managerial Objectives	All managers twice in superior-manager pairs. Once as subordinate then as superior	$\frac{1}{2}$ day
Corporate Objectives Meeting	Organisational Policies, Strategy and Objectives	Top team only once	3 days

Figure 30   The route to effective MBO

(*The four events, in some form or another, are necessary for a sound MBO implementation*)

The team objectives meeting is a three day meeting attended by a superior and all of his subordinates. Teams usually make a large number of important changes at this meeting and finish with a set of well aligned effectiveness areas, effectiveness standards and objectives as well as many plans for improvement. This meeting is described in Chapter 14.

The four hour managerial objectives meeting, the subject of Chapter 15, is a meeting between manager and superior to agree on objectives for the manager. All managers attend this meeting once with their superior and once with each of their subordinates.

The corporate objectives meeting is attended only by the top team and it ends with a skeletal long range plan. It is described in Chapter 16.

The next four chapters deal with the introduction of MBO at managerial, team, pair and corporate level. The frame around each chapter is each of the four courses just described. The chapters are written in such a way, however, that any manager, not just those involved in Effective MBO, can learn and apply the ideas in them and this is especially so for the first three of the four.

New concepts introduced – Chapter 12

CO-WORKER:

> A person with whom a manager works who is neither his superior nor a subordinate.

INSTRUMENTATION:

> A training method which minimises the instructor's role by the use of prework, task assignments and self-generated performance feedback.

MANAGER:

> A person occupying a position in a formal organisation who is responsible for the work of at least one other person and who has formal authority over that person.

ORGANISATION:

> All the factors which influence behaviour within a social system that are common to essentially unrelated positions.

SUBORDINATE:

> A person over whom a manager has authority and for whose work he is responsible.

SUPERIOR:

> A person having authority over a manager and who is responsible for the manager's work.

13 Managerial MBO Implementation

The first question is 'Do I want to become more effective?' The last is 'What can I do now?'

MBO reduces the number of files filled with alibi paper.

Managerial deadwood was alive once; the question is 'What killed it?'

Managers must learn MBO before they are asked to use it so the managerial objectives seminar was designed as the primary method by which Effective MBO is introduced to all managers in the firm.

The objective of the seminar is the clarification of the suitability of a manager's existing effectiveness, areas and effectiveness standards, and his objectives. In addition to its emphasis on effectiveness, it teaches the methods of Effective MBO and shows how a manager may work with it to obtain optimum effectiveness. Participants are grouped into teams of four to eight. The teams are composed of managers who have no current reporting relationships. Most of the seminar time is spent by these teams in working together. This book is the seminar text which is studied in detail by all participants prior to the seminar.

The seminar emphasises effectiveness as the central issue in management. One full day of the seminar is spent solely in each team reaching agreement on the effectiveness areas for each team member. Most managers on this day discover that there is more potential for contribution in their job than they had considered.

At the conclusion of the seminar, the manager is usually highly conscious of himself as a key figure in a situation where effectiveness could be increased. He is usually more open to change. He sees himself, rather than others, as a key to greater effectiveness. He is capable of applying an increased number of sound MBO principles and techniques to achieve effectiveness.

Even when conducted by a company for its own managers the seminar is usually conducted off company premises. About $12\frac{1}{2}$ to 15 per cent of the total work force attend. A company of 1,000 employees would have over 100 take the course. The chairman or managing director usually attends all the in-company seminars for two hours on the last day and solicits comments by giving each team the task of identifying major opportunities for effectiveness within the organisation.

The managerial objectives seminar specifically does not, and could not by itself, introduce MBO into a firm. It does, however, give every manager knowledge about MBO, knowledge about his own effectiveness, and most important, a preparedness to confront the questions below, to answer them, and to take the necessary action. Many of these questions are part of the extensive pre-work for the seminar and all are discussed at it in an open and candid way.

They are given here for the reader to ask and answer for himself.

What are my effectiveness areas now?
Should I try to change my effectiveness areas?
What are my effectiveness standards?
What are my objectives?
How can I improve my superior's effectiveness?
How can I improve my co-workers' effectiveness?
How can I improve my subordinates' effective-
ness?
Should I be doing this?
How can I manage time?
Am I making decisions?
Should I change my job?
What is my future?
What can I do now?

13.1 What are my effectiveness areas now?

The contribution possible from a managerial position is reflected in the effectiveness areas for that position. Clearly, an early step in becoming effective is to establish effectiveness areas. At any level they must be worked out with the superior or they may be meaningless, unacceptable, incorrect, or difficult to apply. Some managers, particularly those at the top of an organisation, find that their areas could take a number of different forms. Setting them then becomes making a decision about what kind of contribution can best be made.

13.2 Should I try to change my effectiveness areas?

If a manager can add a new subordinate position and can define the new subordinate's effectiveness areas, then his own effectiveness areas, as influenced by technology, are capable of wide variation. Within limits he is able to change the things he does or at least the things he places emphasis on. This presents him with one of his most important opportunities to improve effectiveness.

Some freedom is needed to do this, of course, and it is more likely to be found in managers at the top of the organisation or in firms which have a deliberate policy of job flexibility.

Effectiveness areas are particularly susceptible to change in any of these situations: when the job is new, when the manager is new in it, when some kind of crisis situation has developed, and when managers operate as a team and are thus willing to engage in flexible job trading.

13.3 What are my effectiveness standards?

Converting his effectiveness areas to effectiveness standards is a necessary step for any manager to take prior to setting objectives. In establishing effectiveness standards a manager needs to discover what measuring methods are available or can be created. Preparing effectiveness standards also involves him in writing his outputs in concrete terms. Doing the jump direct from effectiveness areas into objectives is a common mistake to make. It omits a rigorous step and one that is necessary if successful alignment is to follow later.

13.4 What are my objectives?

Effectiveness standards are converted to annual objectives. These are the specific, measurable, time-bounded contributions that the manager plans to make.

The superior must always agree to them, co-workers should have an opportunity to comment on them, and subordinates should at least be aware of them.

Objectives which are set for the first time are seldom met. This may reflect either the substitution of hope for reality or simply lack of skill. MBO, like most other skills, requires coaching, training, practice, and feedback on results.

13.5 How can I improve my superior's effectiveness?

Most managers would like to be able to influence their superior in some way. There is no better way for a manager to gain such influence than by amply satisfying his superior's expectations. This usually directly involves the manager in becoming effective and also in making the superior more effective at the same time.

If a manager's own subordinates could take actions to improve his effectiveness, then presumably the manager himself could do the same for his superior. A subordinate is unlikely to do much in the way of changing his superior's style, but he can make his superior more effective. This is particularly possible if the status and the power differential between them are low.

179

A superior may also be influenced by the manager using an indirect approach. In effect, someone else tells him. This influence may be exerted by another manager, a book or article, a consultant, or a course. The written word is a much under-used influence device, yet it is particularly helpful in the low-power situation in which a subordinate usually finds himself.

13.6 How can I improve my co-workers' effectiveness?

Co-workers are usually more open to influence at committee meetings. Managers should therefore think of starting meetings with questions of one of these kinds: 'What is the objective of this meeting?' 'What are its effectiveness areas?' 'Do we need it?' 'Can we conclude it in fifteen minutes?' To do this out of the blue is not always to be recommended, but managers should get around to it as soon as they can.

Over a period of time it is a relatively simple matter for an effective manager to raise the aspiration level of his co-workers. He shares with them their past successes and failures, he can state things as they really are, he can suggest that objectives could be much higher, and by personal example he can show that this is what he intends to do.

13.7 How can I improve my subordinates' effectiveness?

By improving his subordinates' effectiveness a manager also improves his own effectiveness. Perhaps the single best test of a manager is the effectiveness of his subordinates. As a minimum this would be expressed by the capacity for one or two of the subordinates to step into the manager's shoes.

The most effective way of making subordinates more effective is to give them challenging responsibilities early in their careers. The more challenging the responsibilities, the more effective the subordinate is likely to become. Also, clear effectiveness standards for subordinates are obviously crucial.

While the development of managers can be furthered by formal courses, 95 per cent of all real management development goes on in the context of the superior-subordinate relationship. The quality of this relationship determines effectiveness. The superior has by far the most influence in structuring it.

A subordinate does not have to model himself on his superior in order to become effective. But the younger ones tend to do so, especially if the superior appears to be effective, has upward influence and gives them support. Managers usually accept or even welcome such modelling; but the real skill is in recognising, accepting and managing differences. Managers can be effective in different ways. To force a subordinate into his manager's mould may not work or may not be necessary. A superior is not running a game called 'How to Be More Like Me'. He must demonstrate that subordinates should meet their effectiveness standards, not to please him but because their position demands it.

13.8 Should I be doing this?

An effective manager asks of every piece of work that comes before him, 'Who below me could do this?' He does not work himself out of a job in this way; rather, he works himself into his right job. He may well work himself out of routine administration and into long range planning, liaison with other divisions, or the more effective development of his subordinates.

13.9 How can I manage time?

Time, as the economists might put it, is an inelastic resource. You cannot stretch it out. It appears to exist in unlimited quantities in the future, but reaching into the future for it means delay. Time management, perhaps more than anything, is the one skill a manager needs to learn.

Time management starts with a heightened awareness of

time: how much time is available, and how is it being spent? Some managers have found it useful to undertake a study of their own time utilisation. They are almost invariably surprised at the results and the lack of effective time-management displayed.

Effective managers need to learn how to create massed undisturbed time and distributed undisturbed time.

Massed undisturbed time is particularly useful for projects that involve thinking sequentially, such as writing a report, developing a plan, or reading a report or book. Small blocks of distributed undisturbed time are useful for clearing the desk of the accumulation of notices, memos, and travel claims to sign.

An easy short term way to create mass undisturbed time is to come in three hours early or to do work at home. This may lower effectiveness in the long run, so other methods may have to be used. One such method, and there are practical limits in many jobs, is simply to make oneself unavailable on certain days or between certain hours. Most daily interruptions, for many managers, are often on relatively trivial matters. As each interruption occurs, a manager should ask himself, 'How could this have been avoided?', and then modify the decision or information system so that such interruptions either do not occur or at least are minimised.

13.10 Am I making decisions?

Effectiveness can never be brought about unless the right decisions are made. Decisions are a manager's stock in trade. A lack of decision-making can lead to prolonged low effectiveness.

Managers, in reviewing their decisions, often find that most of them could have been made months or years before. Timing is obviously as important as accuracy.

At any one point in time a manager usually has several important decisions he should make. On some, action is postponed for good reasons; on others, it is postponed for perhaps no reason at all. There is no value in making decisions hastily or too far in advance. But there is often no point in postponing them too long, either. Many managers avoid making difficult decisions and let the situation take care of itself over time.

Managers might well prepare a list of all the decisions facing them. This is not the usual list of things to do. It is a decision list with data about each item on which a decision has to be made. The list should have the most pressing decision, which is not necessarily the most important, at the top. This list can be used as a guide to action. With such a list, there is a great temptation to make it and then ignore it, or to make it and then start with the easiest decision rather than the most pressing one.

13.11 Should I change my job?

Once they have looked closely at what a job really demands some managers decide that they are in the wrong job. Sometimes everyone knows it and sometimes no one does. There is a big difference between having daily deadlines and not having them, between supervising professionals and supervising hourly paid workers, between system management and selling. It may be that the job is too demanding, not demanding enough, too boring or involving a manager in things he would simply rather not do.

When one has seen hundreds of managers at work, it takes very little skill to pick the ones who are in the wrong job. They simply are not with it. They get no pleasure out of it. They spend all the time they can doing routine work and avoiding decisions. They are more to be pitied than blamed, but they cannot be ignored. Perhaps the salary attracted them, and that, together with the pension scheme, now has them locked in. Perhaps the job demands changed while they were in it. Perhaps, through their own low sensitivity, they did not know what they were getting into. Take the case of the professional who gets promoted into managing his fellow professionals: a good scientist becomes an unhappy manager.

The ideal solution to this is obvious: change the job. A clear parallel is the college student who switches from one faculty to another. Prior to the switch he is in a turmoil of doubt. After it, he wonders how he could have considered anything else. The majority of managers who move from, or are moved from, a position in which they were performing poorly turn out to be more effective and happy in the new position.

13.12 What is my future?

Whether or not the organisation has a career plan for him, a manager should have one of his own. A manager needs to sit down annually and plan where he expects to be in ten years' time. A good start is to list the ages of all your family at that time, your estimated personal investments, your position, your salary and your accomplishments. Then fill in the ten year gap with what it is necessary for you to do in order to achieve your plan. The future can simply occur or it can be invented. The way the effective manager sees himself must be clear if he is to invent his future.

13.13 What can I do now?

Managers are encouraged to take immediate action after the seminar – as the reader is also encouraged to now. The first step would be to list some specific actions to take and some decisions to make and then to rank them in the order of priority. The basis of the priority would be the extent to which each would make you more effective. As a minimum you may wish to consider:

> Establishing your effectiveness areas
> Giving parts of your job to others
> Structuring your time use differently

13.14 The big step to the team

After a manager has learned MBO from the managerial objectives seminar he is asked to put it to use with his full team. The team objectives meeting is the method used.

New concept introduced – Chapter 13

MANAGERIAL OBJECTIVES SEMINAR (MOS):
A seminar conducted in-company or publicly where managers without line relationships to each other learn Effective MBO.

14 Team MBO Implementation

There are only two occasions on which to use participation; one is when the decision will be improved with it, and the other is when commitment will be improved with it.

Teamwork is not a 'groupy' activity where responsibility is blurred – it is the opposite in fact.

The biggest gap in current MBO implementation is the lack of use of the work unit or team to facilitate the change. Most MBO implementations are based on a one-to-one design, where a superior speaks to each of his subordinates in turn. Virtually no MBO technique even tries to get the full team together, superior and all subordinates, to work out effectiveness areas, objectives, and improvement plans as a group.

One reason why these meetings are avoided is the fear of disagreement. Another is that early attempts were not predictable as to outcome. What was needed was a device to train a team as a unit which was always safe and usually effective. In response to this need, the team objectives meeting was developed. It has been under continuous test and revision as the Team Role Laboratory for ten years. It is now widely used.

Teamwork in industry is clearly acceptable. This is Drucker's view of almost twenty years ago:

> In business, teams are used a good deal more than the literature indicates. They are regularly employed for short-term assignments in every large company. They are common in research work. Team organisation, rather than the hierarchy of rank shown on the organisation chart, is the reality in the well-run manufacturing plant, especially in respect to the relationship between the plant

manager and the heads of the technical functions reporting to him. Many tasks in process manufacturing or in mass production new style can only be done if organised on a team basis.

He clarifies the view that teamwork depends on clear objectives and responsibilities:

> It is therefore of genuine importance that management understand what team organisation is, when to use it, and how. Above all, it is important that management realise that in any real team each member has a clearly assigned and clearly defined role. A team is not just chaos made into a virtue. Teamwork requires actually more internal organisation, more co-operation, and greater definiteness of individual assignments than work organised in individual jobs.

It is hardly reasonable not to share his view today.

Teamwork is not a 'groupy' activity where everyone does his own thing and responsibility is blurred. Members of a football team or a mountaineering team all have clear roles, clear effectiveness areas, and a clear leader. We still call them 'teams', and appropriately so. All efforts are directed to common team objectives, not individual objectives.

There is little question that a manager's co-workers, his peers, are in an excellent position to tell him how best to improve his effectiveness. The difficulty is, how can conditions be created where they will tell him and where he will listen? Conditions of increased trust must be established. Between them the managerial objectives seminar and the team objectives meeting actually produce these conditions.

In the three-day team objectives meeting, a manager and all his subordinate managers discuss their objectives and decide how best to improve the way they work together. The team objectives meeting has been described as situational management for a team and also as a work-study conference for a team. Each of these descriptions does reflect the essence of the design. The emphasis is not on personality or subordinates' rating of their superior, but on individual and unit effectiveness areas. The team objectives meeting is usually conducted by company or external trainers.

After about twenty hours of pre-work has been completed by each team member, the meeting is held. The meeting requires each team member, including the top man, to read out his effectiveness areas, describing what programmes he follows to meet them and then specifying what each team member could do for him that would enable him to improve his managerial effectiveness. Another key activity is the design of an optimal organisation chart for the team or department. This single activity almost always leads to a structural change which is often long overdue and definitely needed before effectiveness can increase.

The team objectives meeting leads directly to a clear definition of the team's role in the organisation. With this established, team effectiveness areas and team objectives may be prepared. Often the preparation requires some type of team reorganisation, which the team designs and implements. Flexible job trading usually occurs and leads to the talents of individual managers being better utilised through job enrichment. Needless to say, the enthusiasm and commitment generated by this activity leads to the solution of many problems.

The team objectives meeting takes place only after all team members have participated in the managerial objectives seminar. The seminar induces a readiness to change, for which the team objectives meeting provides the vehicle.

The use of the team objectives meeting avoids such clumsy attempts at MBO implementation as are represented by this comment.

> As was to be expected, the reception of this process varied enormously from one individual to another. Some people took to it like ducks to water, others most reluctantly. Some of the initial encounters between manager and adviser took as long as 12 hours before the adviser was able to wring out of the 'subject' an admission that his affairs could be improved. Little wonder

that from time to time an adviser would be downcast, but sooner or later a breakthrough would be achieved which would lift him to a state of near euphoria.

14.1 The team objectives meeting programme

About eight weeks prior to the meeting each team member, including the superior, receives a thirty-two page booklet containing the pre-work for the team objectives meeting. The participants are told it will take from fifteen to twenty hours to do this pre-work. All pre-work is completed privately by each team member without consultation. All complete identical pre-work.

These notes taken from the pre-work give an idea of the orientation supplied.

> Your team has decided that it wants to undertake a team development project known as the 'team objectives meeting'. This meeting is attended by all team members and lasts for three or four full days. The objective of the meeting is to help the team to improve its effectiveness.
>
> During the meeting, the team members remain together for the whole time. Early morning starts and late night finishes are common.
>
> All the discussion at the meeting is team property. It is thus as confidential or as public as the team wishes.
>
> As indicated elsewhere, this pre-work is to be completed well before the meeting itself and mailed to the person who will be assisting your team at the meeting in improving its operations. Only he, and possibly an assistant, will see your pre-work before it is returned to you intact at the start of the meeting. During the meeting, all of the pre-work is shared by the team as a whole.

In the early use of team objective meetings in an organisation, the person conducting a particular team objectives meeting will usually visit the team to discuss the pre-work. As more managers participate in them, all managers get to know those who have completed one and thus a consultant's visit is not necessary to explain it. Team objectives meetings start at the top, so that a manager's superior has already participated in one as a subordinate.

The objectives of the meeting are given as:

1 To decide the team's actual role in the organisation and how it might best contribute to overall effectiveness.
2 To explore the job of each team member and to agree on the method by which his effectiveness should be judged.
3 To decide on an optimal team organisation.
4 To decide how the team will make future decisions.
5 To decide on key specific team objectives to be accomplished in the next six to twelve months.

And team members are invited to suggest other objectives. When these objectives are discussed at the start of the meeting, team members usually have nothing to add and say something like, 'If we can get all that lot done, it will be enough'.

14.2 The tasks of the pre-work

The fifteen tasks are listed in the pre-work as:

1 Introduction and objectives
2 Team member effectiveness areas
3 Unit effectiveness areas
4 Optimal team organisation
5 Team improvement objectives
6 Team member effectiveness
7 Team effectiveness evaluation
8 Team meeting improvements
9 Team decision making
10 Job rotation plan
11 Committee structure plan
12 Project team plan
13 Managerial objectives meeting

14 Consultant observations
15 Senior manager review

All participants are required to complete all tasks which are assigned. The pre-work is essentially identical for all levels in

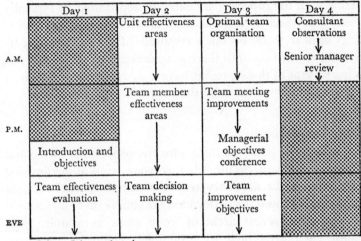

	Day 1	Day 2	Day 3	Day 4
A.M.		Unit effectiveness areas ↓	Optimal team organisation ↓	Consultant observations ↓ Senior manager review ↓
P.M.	Introduction and objectives	Team member effectiveness areas ↓	Team meeting improvements ↓ Managerial objectives conference	
EVE	Team effectiveness evaluation ↓	Team decision making ↓	Team improvement objectives ↓	

Other: Job rotation plan
Committee structure plan
Project team plan

Figure 31   Team objectives meeting schedule

(*This four-day meeting brings a management team together to discuss its effectiveness and its objectives*)

an organisation except for three tasks. The tasks of 'Job rotation plan', 'Committee structure plan' and 'Project team plan' usually apply only to higher levels.

A typical four-day schedule, using these tasks, is shown in Figure 31.

14.2.1 *Introduction and objectives*

14.2.2 *Team member effectiveness areas*
After the introduction task comes the team member effectiveness area task, which asks: 'List below in point form the effectiveness areas on which you could, or actually do, set your objectives

191

and by which you determine how well you personally are fulfilling the responsibilities of your own function. Each of the effectiveness areas should be expressed in one to four words and conditional indicators, such as *increase* may be omitted.'

At the meeting, the effectiveness areas of each team member starting with the superior, are carefully scrutinised. It typically occurs that there is a great deal of overlap and that some things appear to be no one's responsibility. The effectiveness areas are worked on until there is agreement. At the end of this session several of those present have a sharply changed view of their job, which is shared by their superior and co-workers.

14.2.3 *Unit effectiveness areas*
The next task concerns unit effectiveness areas: 'By what criteria would you decide whether your team is performing well? What is the necessary area of accomplishment? Against what criteria should the performance of your team be measured? List the effectiveness areas of your team as a unit. Note against each area how its attainment could be measured accurately.'

Strangely enough, this question has often never been discussed before by the unit. In staff groups particularly there is an enormous distortion about what the role should be. At one meeting this task alone led directly to a complete realignment of the staff role in a 1,000 man division.

14.2.4 *Optimal team organisation*
One of the most important tasks in the meeting is: 'As companies grow, organisation charts often become outmoded and are not in keeping with the true needs of the company, or with modern management practice. Your task is to devise the best organisation structure that your team should aim for within the near future. Assume that the changes you propose could be made over a year or so. Assume also that qualified management is available, or could be trained, to assume any new or modified job functions you might create. Be as creative as possible. Consider only those jobs over which your team's

top member or the team itself has control. This may involve several levels.'

Most superiors are under the impression that only minor changes will arise. The opposite is usually what happens. While these figures are only rough, this is a frequency distribution of changes that occurred in one company.

No changes	10%
Add or remove a position	80%
Split into two or more units	15%
Add or remove a layer	20%
Abandon team	5%

The team abandonment occurs when all positions are moved to other parts of the organisation.

For those who doubt the value of such sessions as these, sitting in while this one task is discussed would remove any such doubt.

14.2.5 *Team improvement objectives*

Another task with enormous payoff is: 'If your team worked at a high level of effectiveness over the next year, what specific problems would it have solved? The problems identified should be those which, if solved, would enable the team to do better work in achieving its objectives. These may relate to technical training, management training, job rotation, resource allocation, project priorities, planning, staffing, career planning, costing, pricing, cost-benefit analyses. Many of these problems may have appeared and reappeared as agenda items. They may be frequently talked about and never solved; they may have been put aside as too difficult to solve; they may have been accepted by some as virtually insoluble.'

Among them, the members of a team would typically produce a list of thirty to forty important, not trite, items. At the meeting the team is asked to pick the most important of the items and set an objective concerning each and a plan for improvement.

14.2.6 *Team member effectiveness*
The team member effectiveness task is in three parts:

Top member changes. 'What could your top member do personally that would allow you to improve your effectiveness without lowering his?'

Team member changes. 'What could each of the other team members do that would allow you to improve your own or your division's or department's effectiveness without lowering his own? Some of your suggestions, for instance, may be based on changes in operating policy that another member could initiate for his department or divison. It is important to list as many as possible of the helpful actions that individual team members could take. You may wish to go into some detail on this topic and take a great deal of time with it.'

Personal changes. 'What could you do personally to improve your effectiveness and that of your team without lowering the effectiveness of someone else? If you wish, specify what you could do for the *team* as a whole, for the *top member* and for each specific *team member*.'

A guide is provided which gives ideas on the typical changes suggested:

Top member changes
   Information flow, communication
   Controls, procedures
   Aspects of his or your method of organising, planning, evaluation, or setting objectives
   Co-operation, conflict

Team member changes
   Aspects of each team member's work oganisation and planning
   Information flow, communication
   Co-operation, conflict

Personal changes
   Information flow, communication
   Co-operation, conflict
   Aspects of your organisation, planning, evaluation, control
      methods, etc.

When specific suggestions are made for changes, the manager to whom they are directed is required to say whether or not he will make the change. If he says 'no' he is required to explain why. This task highlights the interdependence of team members and leads to much higher co-operation.

14.2.7 *Team effectiveness evaluation*
The team's effectiveness is then rated. 'Rate your team over the past six months or so on a study of Team Effectiveness.' This task looks at how well the team, as a whole, is fulfilling its effectiveness areas. The emphasis is on the team as a whole, not on the individuals in it.

The scales on which the team rates itself are: creativity, data collection, setting objectives, planning, introducing change, implementation, productivity, and evaluation.

This frank look at unit effectiveness is sometimes a surprise to a complacent top man who thought everything was perfect.

14.2.8 *Team meeting improvements*
Teams get into poor working habits, and the task on the team meeting itself is very useful. It reads:

> Over years of working together most teams follow operating habits and working procedures which either were not well planned originally or which become outmoded as the team matures and grows. A few examples of such practices concern: frequency and timing of meetings, membership of meetings, items discussed at meetings (for decision) (for information), the content, form and frequency of reports and controls, specific standard operating procedures directly affecting the team, method

of allocating projects and assignments, method of determining project priorities, how changes are introduced, method of communicating decisions. They are then asked to list, in point form, the issues they would like to raise about the way the team works together.

The directions of the outputs of this task depend on team needs; the outputs have no general direction. Some teams move to greater, and some to less, formality. Some teams increase meeting frequency and some reduce the frequency of meetings. What always happens is that the team decides when it should meet, about what, and under what conditions.

14.2.9 *Team decision making*

The distribution of power in the team is an important issue to air. A variety of methods can work, but all the team members should agree on what the methods are and when they should be used. The pre-work contains this information:

'There are five methods by which components of teams may be used in decision making. These are:

A. *One-only.* In the *one-only* method the top member alone makes the decision and announces it to the team.

B. *One-one.* In the *one-one* method the top member obtains the suggestions of a single team member. He bases his decision, in part, on the suggestions he receives from the single member.

C. *One-team.* In the *one-team* method the top member obtains suggestions and ideas at one time from all team members affected by the decision. He bases his decision largely on the suggestions he receives from all team members.

D. *Majority.* In the *majority* method the decision is put to a vote and the majority vote decides.

E. *Consensus.* In the *consensus* method the team as a unit shares its information, suggestions, and ideas and, as a team, reaches a decision through obtaining consensus.

All of these methods are appropriate from time to time. For some decisions the low participation *one-only* method is appropriate, and sometimes one of the other successively higher participation methods should be used. The more effective manager would make use of all of them.

Team members are asked to estimate what percentage each method is used concerning important matters affecting the team, and also to estimate what they think the preferred percentage should be.

This task then enables the team to get directly at the issue of power and decision making practices. If power is too diffuse or too concentrated this issue is always well aired and, in most cases, improvements are made. Here again, the direction of an improvement depends on the team. Some teams ask the superior to make more decisions. Other teams ask the opposite.

Next are three other tasks which are assigned only at more senior levels where they apply.

14.2.10 *Job rotation plan*
'Would lateral job rotation of some members of your team, or of those at lower levels, lead to improved managerial effectiveness? If so, recommend an initial set of job rotation candidates.'

14.2.11 *Committee structure plan*
'What changes would you like to see in the structure of the standing committees which report to your team and over which your team has control? If your team has no standing committees associated with it you may wish to propose new standing committees, if you believe they would lead to improved effectiveness.'

14.2.12 *Project team plan*
'It is sometimes advisable to establish project teams to investigate, and usually to give recommendations concerning, special subjects which cut across functional areas or which require concentrated or long-term effort. Membership on these teams

is selected on a "capacity to solve" basis rather than to represent special interests. If you believe that one or more such teams would be desirable, specify the subject to be investigated.'

These tasks alone can initiate changes which greatly affect the units effectiveness.

14.2.13 *Managerial objectives meeting*
The consultant then outlines the managerial objectives meeting. He distributes the work for it and suggests that each team member soon selects a date to hold the meeting with the team's top member.

14.2.14 *Consultant observations*
Near the end of the meeting, the consultant makes his observations about the team. He comments on how he thought they handled each task, the outstanding work still to be done, and the unresolved problems still facing the team. The consultant is trained to be frank and not to leave things unsaid.

14.2.15 *Senior manager review*
For the last hour of the meeting the superior's superior arrives. He sits with the team and asks, 'What have you decided?' By the time he arrives, all walls of the meeting room are plastered with paper, and improvement plans are sketched out, together with the effectiveness areas of individuals. The proposed revision of the organisation chart often has pride of place.

In about 95 per cent of the cases the superior's superior has already participated in a team objectives meeting. This will not only prepare him for the kinds of changes proposed but also create open and candid conditions for discussion.

Success rate. About nine out of ten team objectives meetings are clearly successful. On the last day everyone present knows that it has been an important experience. About one in ten teams do not 'make it'. This almost always takes the form of a quiet team objectives meeting at which nothing but minor changes are made. This condition arises most often when the superior is not open to any kinds of change and the subordinates do not care to propose them.

The most important outputs of the team objectives meeting are:

> The team role is better defined
> Team effectiveness areas are established
> Team improvement objectives are established
> Team is reorganised if it needs it
> Managerial effectiveness areas are established
> Team decision making is improved
> Talents of individuals are better used
> Individual jobs are enriched
> Motivation increases sharply
> There is clearly greater team and managerial effectiveness

Job and Unit Effectiveness descriptions. Soon after the team objectives meeting, the job effectiveness descriptions and the unit effectiveness description should be formally written. Typically, the team objectives meeting does not have time enough to do this formally and an expert outsider is useful. After these are written the team usually comes together for a day to discuss and approve them. For the more senior teams the outsider is usually an MBO consultant, from outside the company. He trains an internal MBO specialist who is a company employee and who assists lower level teams with their job and unit effectiveness descriptions.

New concept introduced – Chapter 14

TEAM OBJECTIVES MEETING (TOM):
> A three-day meeting between a manager and all his subordinates at which unit and individual effectiveness areas are established and appropriate changes made in unit organisation structure, policies, and procedures.

15 One-to-One MBO Implementation

Ninety five per cent of MBO and of management development must occur in the context of the superior-subordinate relationship.

The true title of too many appraisal interviews is 'how to be more like me'.

The best way to change your superior's methods is first to meet his objectives in your job as he sees them.

Within a few months of his participation in the team objectives meeting a manager participates in a managerial objectives meeting. This is a two-man meeting between a manager and his superior. This meeting, once held, then becomes a regular event. It strengthens the superior-subordinate relationship around objective setting. It has many differences from the designs of other such sessions, particularly the high degree of information on both sides arising from the team objectives meeting, the behavioural basis of the design, the emphasis on removing blockages and, a major difference, that the manager not the superior does most of the pre-work – and the talking.

While this chapter is specifically about the managerial objectives meeting most of it is of direct assistance to anyone wishing to improve his coaching practices. To review other methods first:

15.1 Who drafts objectives?

There are four widely used methods of drafting the initial set of objectives. These are summarised in Figure 32. One method is for the superior simply to hand the objectives to the manager;

another is for the superior to draft them initially and then discuss them with the manager; the third method is for the manager to draft them initially and discuss them with his superior; the fourth method is for the manager and the MBO specialist to draft them and then for both to discuss them at a meeting with the manager's superior. This fourth method is the best method

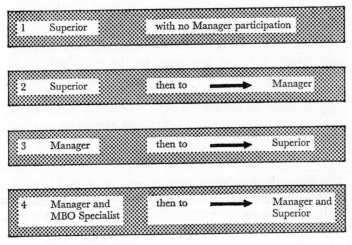

Figure 32   Who drafts objectives?
(*The four ways of arriving at objectives; the last two are better*)

and is the design of the managerial objectives meeting (MOM) which is the main topic of this chapter.

The first method, then, is for the superior to draft objectives for the manager. This, at first sight, seems the obvious way to do things and is still used by some. The problem with this is that it is not much more than giving a more specific order than usual. It certainly does not contain all the elements of planning, involvement and commitment implied by MBO. A major weakness of this method is that it does not tap the manager's ideas or develop him, and it certainly does not get him involved. It is essentially MBO by edict.

The second method involves the superior drafting the objectives and then discussing them with the manager. This method is specifically proposed in one MBO book: it goes this far:

> Here, then, are the completed tentative objectives the boss has decided upon for this manager:
>
> 1 Increase unit sales of product lines as follows:
>   - (*a*) Toasters: 14 per cent
>   - (*b*) Waffle irons: 8 per cent
>   - (*c*) Frying pans: 26 per cent
> 2 Increase by 9 per cent the number of successful recommendations provided to the new-business unit, both for new dealers and for extending the present lines sold by established dealers.
> 3 Reduce by 30 per cent the number of cases in which dealer and customer complaints cannot be resolved by salesmen or by the sales manager.
> 4 Reduce sales costs by 4 per cent.
>
> Now the boss's preliminary work on the objectives for this manager is done . . . he will be prepared to enter into his discussions . . . knowing that he is ready to contribute his share in the joint task of deciding on firm objectives.

The idea is that all of the objectives are tentative and thus open for change and discussion. This is better than the first method, but the weakness is that the superior quickly finds himself defending what have become his objectives rather than the manager's. Also, the good ideas of the manager are not best tapped. Commitment again is unlikely to result.

While the author leaves some opportunity for discussion by the subordinate, it is clear that he prefers top down objective setting with little or no reference to the company plan. For an inexperienced subordinate, this might be appropriate. For an experienced one, it assumes he must be a dull clod. If the superior can draft the objective, why can't the subordinate do it equally well? They can each have access to the same parts of the corporate objectives from which managerial objectives must flow.

There is a great deal of misunderstanding and the declaration of many platitudes concerning whether objectives should come from the superior or from the subordinate. The question is asked the wrong way. Objectives flow from corporate strategy, and both superior and subordinate should contribute as much as they can at the appropriate time. Participation should always be used if subordinates can contribute to making a decision better. It should also be used if their commitment to the objective is important and if this commitment can be increased by participation. The latter condition is almost always present.

The third method is for the manager to draft a set of proposed objectives and, sometimes over a series of several meetings, work out with his superior what his objectives should be.

This method is recommended by one writer:

> Experience has proved that the best method of setting objectives is the one in which the objectives are drafted and recommended by the individual managers and then approved by their superiors. Setting his own objectives . . . requires the manager to determine how his department fits into the company as a whole, size up its strong and weak points, determine its total capability, and reach his own conclusions. It permits him to exercise his own ingenuity and initiative.

By use of this method both sides can contribute fairly evenly to the objectives and both will then have a thorough understanding of what the drafted objectives mean and imply. Because of inexperience on both sides, the initial objectives so drafted will not be perfect. Of far more importance, however, will be the joint commitment to a start. The difficulty with this plan in practice is that it requires each manager to understand thoroughly all the ideas behind effectiveness areas. This requirement can, of course, be accomplished, but it may, in the long run, be unnecessary training.

Method four is widely used to establish objectives. It adds a third party, an internal or external MBO specialist, who meets privately with the manager on request, and then, possibly, also jointly with the manager and his superior, to help them obtain agreement to a set of effectiveness areas, objectives and measurement methods. The major advantages of using a third party are his added experience, his perceived impartiality, and the tendency for objectives to be established because a man has been hired to see to it.

The staff specialist must be well trained or even this excellent method can be weakened. If the staff man is not sensitive to overall capacity and the capacity to change, the initial set of objectives sometimes tends to be more sophisticated than either the superior or the manager can handle. Or the manager, knowing who is paying the staff man, can sometimes see the meeting as a two against one proposition. Rather than spontaneous involvement being elicited from the subordinate, suppressed hostility or passive acceptance can occur. The manager can feel he is being got at, and thus he may want to protect himself. One purpose of MBO is to strengthen the superior-manager relationship. A third party must be adroit so as not to inhibit this result taking place.

15.2 The managerial objectives meeting

The managerial objectives meeting is a four- to eight-hour meeting between a manager and his superior. Both the manager and the superior have pre-work to do. The manager's pre-work may take him from ten to twenty hours and is all job related. If he wishes, he may have the assistance of the MBO staff specialist in doing it. The superior's pre-work takes him about one to two hours per subordinate. The managerial objectives meeting is followed by a series of regular, usually quarterly, checkpoint meetings, at which progress toward objectives is reviewed.

The design of the meeting may be summarised this way:

Managerial objectives meeting design
Who: Between a superior and each of the managers
        reporting to him in one-to-one meetings.

What:	A discussion of effectiveness areas, effectiveness standards, objectives, and blockages.
Objective:	To agree on the manager's objectives.
When:	Whenever needed, usually annually with quarterly checkpoint meetings.
Where:	In the manager's office or in a conference room.

The MOM pre-work is printed in a booklet with spaces for the superior and manager to do their pre-work and record their consensus. The booklet is given to and belongs to the manager, not the superior. When the manager is ready to participate in a managerial objectives meeting he removes a section from his booklet that is intended for the superior's use, and selects the date with him.

To outline clearly the design of this meeting and the associated activities, each of these topics will be taken up in turn.

> The manager's pre-work
> The superior's pre-work
> The managerial objectives meeting agenda
> The checkpoint meeting
> The managerial objectives meeting cycle
> Paperwork and records
> The value of the managerial objectives meeting
> A comparison with traditional appraisal

15.2.1 *The manager's pre-work*
The manager's pre-work for the managerial objectives meeting requires him to make what are essentially seven lists of his views on each of:

> 1 Effectiveness areas of his unit
> 2 Effectiveness areas of himself
> 3 Blockages to his effectiveness within the company

205

4 Blockages to his effectiveness between himself and his superior

5 Blockages to his effectiveness within himself

6 His objectives

7 Superior's assistance requested

If the manager has had no prior training in MBO or prior discussion about his unit's role in the company, doing this pre-work well becomes a formidable task. Usually however the manager will have participated in the managerial objectives seminar at which his effectiveness areas were established. He will also have participated in the most important team objectives meeting. At this meeting all the items of managerial objectives meeting pre-work were discussed at length and now the time has come to pin them down.

The effectiveness areas for the unit should have been fairly well established at the team objectives meeting and all the managers in the unit and the superior should have agreed on a single set. The set should be seen as flexible, however, and a constant airing of the selected areas in an attempt to improve them is useful. When a manager is asked to list the effectiveness areas of his unit and his superior, it can slow him in his tracks. This may well be the first time he has been asked to think about them, or has thought about them. In working out these effectiveness areas, the manager usually comes to see himself, his superior, and his unit as important links in a chain to achieve company objectives. He sees that his superior, as well as himself, is subjected to rigorous performance measures. This revelation can assist him to see that MBO is not simply a 'tighten up on subordinates' scheme, but a device for obtaining job clarity and integration.

The manager will usually have worked out his own effectiveness areas, but each year, through the managerial objectives meeting, he is asked to take another look. The job may have changed. The management may have grown in skill, or a better set of effectiveness areas may have been developed for the existing position.

The next three parts of the pre-work allow a manager to

deal directly with perceived blockages to effectiveness which are bothering him. Without this section, managers report, it would be very difficult or impossible really to clear the air so that the managerial objectives meeting really gets off the ground and becomes productive. Even a willingness to list these blockages requires a degree of candour and trust not always present in industrial organisations. The managerial objectives seminar and the team objectives meeting lead directly to these conditions being produced.

The manager moves on to cast his objectives as soundly as possible, together with his measurement methods and programmes of activities. This section will take him the most time and is where he may most need some outside assistance.

Finally the manager lists the superior's assistance he requires. At times this space is left blank. The manager has both a clear road and competence, and he knows it.

15.2.2 *The superior's pre-work*

The superior's pre-work for the managerial objectives meeting requires him to make two lists. In addition, he privately appraises, for his own information, three aspects of the manager's effectiveness. His pre-work is very little indeed. This is an important and deliberate part of the meeting design. The responsibility for objective setting is thrown on to the manager not his superior. The combination of the managerial objectives seminar and team objectives meeting help to ensure that the manager is willing to accept such responsibility.

The two lists are:

1 Effectiveness areas of the unit of which the manager and the superior are part
2 Effectiveness areas of the manager

In addition, the superior considers, in a general way, the manager's:

1 Past effectiveness
2 Blockages to effectiveness

3 Potential for effectiveness

4 Assistance requirement for improved effectiveness

This pre-work will take him about one to two hours per manager.

So, in addition to listing the two sets of effectiveness areas the superior thinks about his managers' past effectiveness, blockages to their effectiveness, their potential for effectiveness, and the assistance required for them to improve their effectiveness. All of these questions concern effectiveness and nothing else. No distracting side issues are raised. The first two questions concerning 'past' and 'blockages', may reveal the problems; the second two concerning 'potential' and 'assistance', may reveal the opportunities.

15.2.3 *The managerial objectives meeting agenda*

The managerial objectives meeting agenda requires the manager and superior together to agree on eight things:

1 Effectiveness areas of unit

2 Effectiveness areas of manager

3 Company blockages to manager

4 Superior-manager blockages

5 Manager's personal blockages

6 Manager's objectives

   (*a*) Priorities of objectives

   (*b*) Methods of measurement for objectives

   (*c*) Programme of activities for objectives (review only)

7 Superior's assistance needed and available

8 Checkpoint meeting time

Two copies of number 6 only are typed later on Objective Record Sheets. Number 7 is recorded separately in the managerial objectives meeting workbook. The total managerial objectives meeting takes about four to eight hours. The first meeting takes the most time.

Naturally enough, the first meeting is often approached

with a little trepidation on both sides. This can be cleared up if both men first agree on the objective of the meeting, its procedure, and what follows after. The procedure is exactly what it says: reach agreement on each item in turn. No two men in the company are better suited to this task.

The *unit effectiveness areas* are usually agreed to fairly quickly if the managerial objectives meeting was preceded by a team objectives meeting; otherwise, this topic may take a long time. It is an imporant question to settle, however, as a manager could not possibly set his objectives without a full understanding of the unit effectiveness areas first. When, as often arises naturally, the effectiveness areas of the superior also get worked out and agreed, some managers have a better insight into blockages they thought existed. Some in fact, on understanding the superior's effectiveness areas more clearly, remove many of the blockages they were going to bring up. This leads naturally to the discussion of the *manager's effectiveness areas*. When these are agreed at least half of the important work at the first managerial objectives meeting is done.

When dealing with *blockages*, both sides should work to eliminate as many as possible, but they should be candid and accept things that cannot be changed. Some company blockages may remain as blockages for ever. And human beings, none of whom are 100 per cent flexible, may have difficulty in changing behaviour which gets them into trouble. First, blockages have to be stated clearly on both sides. Whether or not they can be changed is not the issue at this point. Candour about them is. The superior is usually able to identify some in the three areas mentioned which the manager did not think of.

Once the blockages are identified, then each may be taken in turn and the change possibilities considered. In the discussion of some blockages, an agreement to change may have arisen spontaneously. In others, a searching inquiry will be required. The managerial objectives meeting does not magically remove all blockages. It does identify them, however. It removes some and leaves a recognition on both sides about the others which inhibit effectiveness.

The manager next proposes his *objectives*. Some of these will be modified if the effectiveness areas are changed. The questions both sides will be most concerned with are:

> Are they output?
> Are they measurable?
> Are they ambitious enough?

Priorities are then agreed and measurements for each are decided or agreement is reached to establish them.

The *programme of activities* is the manager's responsibility, not the superior's. The superior who spends too much time looking at activities in the managerial objectives meeting is probably an input orientated bureaucrat. Newer subordinates, of course, will welcome a discussion of their plan but experienced subordinates probably will not need it.

Agreement is then obtained on what *assistance from the superior* will be available. If a superior can say yes to most of his subordinate's requests, he is probably doing his part in ensuring his subordinate's effectiveness.

The manager takes the responsibility for providing two typed sets of the objective record sheet and for supplying one to his superior. A meeting about two weeks away may also be arranged simply to agree on the typed objectives.

The time for a review is selected at the managerial objectives meeting. The review is normally called a *checkpoint* meeting (CPM). The checkpoint should be the most convenient time at which progress toward objectives may be reviewed. While the obvious checkpoint is an objective completion date, this may not always be the best time. Intermediate checks allow a greater opportunity for coaching and review. The checkpoints for many quantitative goals, such as profits, sales, costs, accidents, and quality may be related to the time at which information on these normally becomes available through the company reporting system. A single checkpoint three or six months away may be set, or several checkpoints may be set. For a particular job, checkpoints were established at one, seven, nine and ten months. The manager's major effectiveness areas concerned new product introduction. By the first month, an integrated plan needed review and approval; by the seventh month, the market test would be completed; by the ninth month a national introduction would be fully planned with sales training completed; and by the tenth month, a specified degree of distribution would be obtained. For a new manager with this job, four checkpoints would be appropriate; for an experienced manager, perhaps only one. One every three to four months is normally preferred in the early stages of the introduction of MBO when it is usual to have a high frequency of checkpoints in the first year or two. Not only is progress toward objectives being reviewed, but managers are also learning more about how to use MBO.

Examples of superior's comments at managerial objectives meeting. While the manager does most of the pre-work for the managerial objectives meeting, the superior himself is by no means a passive observer at the meeting. As an illustration of his role, here are the kinds of comments he might make.

'I think the team agreed on the unit effectiveness areas at the team objectives meeting. Shall we work with those, or have you other ideas?'

'Can you give that effectiveness area to a subordinate?'

'You haven't an objective concerning profit improvement in product Y. Do you see it as your job?'

'Let's call Jack in about this as his numerical objective will have to link with yours.'

'Could you make that cost reduction a higher figure? What can you do about staff level, overtime, your floor space and computer time?'

'I agree you do not have authority to make that decision, so that cannot be your objective. How can we frame an objective that does reflect your authority?'

'Things are running pretty smoothly in your department now. Could you swing 25 per cent of your time allocation to innovation? What could you do there?'

'In what one area do you plan to show most improvement?'

'Unless you have a tight measure of customer satisfaction let's throw it out. Can you think of another way of getting at the same idea?'

'This quality level you have set is the same as last year's. Can you bring it down? Do you want help from me?'

'I agree I haven't done enough about telling you how you are doing. What about meeting monthly for a while and going over your progress towards each objective?'

'That company rule is a blockage I agree. You know it is, I know it is and my boss knows it is. At the moment it is a fact of life, though I will continue to try to get it changed.'

'One blockage between us you didn't bring up is my tendency to want things immediately. It is a blockage, I know. I am not saying I can change but I would like to know its impact on you.'

'As you know, the executive committee has a drive this year on meeting deadlines. How can you contribute more than you did last year?'

15.2.4 *The checkpoint meeting*
The function of the checkpoint meeting between a manager and his superior is to review progress towards objectives and to plan corrective action if necessary. It takes one to two hours and is normally held quarterly or half yearly but can be held when needed. The checkpoint meeting makes MBO come to life in an organisation. It makes the whole process real and facilitates an integration of MBO into other organisation systems such as budgeting.

The typed objective record sheets are reviewed and for

each objective at or past its completion date these questions are asked:

> Was the objective met?
> Why was there variance from it, if any?
> Is the measurement method adequate?

The findings are recorded in the 'actual performance' section. And for each other objective:

> Is progress satisfactory?
> Is corrective action needed?
> Is amendment to the objective needed?

And for new objectives:

> Clear statements are made

Two new sets of objective record sheets are typed if needed and the next checkpoint meeting time agreed.

The focus of the checkpoint meeting is naturally the extent to which the objectives have been met and the reasons for under achievement, if any. Several objectives will have been easily met; some will be seen in retrospect as having been impossible to meet.

When objectives are not met. During the early stages of MBO introduction, objectives will frequently not have been met. The rules to follow are complete openness about the degree of attainment, a focus on causes in terms of what was or what was not done, a discussion of any corrections that can be applied immediately, and a decision on how to avoid failure in the future.

In summary, when objectives are not met, consider:

> What was done
> What was not done
> How to correct now
> How to avoid in future

If the objective was not met, the cause should be identified. It may be one of the following:

> Objective too high
> Insufficient resources requested
> Insufficient resources supplied
> Poor planning
> Failure to follow plan established
> Unanticipated events (changed conditions)
> Insufficient motivation
> Too much selling effort devoted to accounts with low potential
> Lack of sales follow-up
> Manager does not work effectively with staff advisers
> High staff turnover in unit – no trained replacements
> Insufficient coaching of subordinates

If the objective was significantly exceeded, an inquiry should also be made. While usually desirable its achievement could have caused problems to others. The following questions are important.

> Was the objective too low initially?
> Why did over achievement occur?
> Can it be repeated?

Checkpoint meeting errors. The managerial objectives meeting itself and the associated checkpoint meeting are designed to eliminate most of the horrors of appraisal schemes and interviews. Many such schemes in industry still are little more than paperwork and are known to have little effect. More and more firms, recognising their lack of effectiveness in changing behaviour, have discontinued the formal appraisal scheme. Fortunately such ideas as MBO and the managerial objectives meeting allow such firms to have another start, this time on the right foot.

The climate in the checkpoint meeting is that of two rational men making a review. When the review finds under achievement, the causes for it are identified so as to reduce the possibility of recurrence. The climate is not one of criticism or even praise. Studies have demonstrated that, as a general rule, neither criticism nor praise improves performance. In fact, criticism reduces performances.

The most common errors at CPMs are:

> Traits or personality discussion
> Emphasis on incidents – nagging
> Hiding own views
> Focus on activities, not results
> Focus on 'no-control' items
> Being too participative
> Being too rigid
> Implied emphasis on 'pleasing me'
> Discussion of salary

A discussion of a manager's personality will not help him change it or improve his performance. It is of no value to tell a manager he 'pushes too hard' or is 'too easy-going'. These things will not change him and he will resent them. He was engaged to perform, not to conform. Discuss performance not personality inputs. The true title of some appraisal interviews is 'How to be more like me'. Some appraisers, in an attempt to drive a point home, keep harping on it. 'If you had not . . .' or 'if only you had. . . .' This doesn't usually work with the children or the wife, why should it work with managers? A checkpoint meeting is an opportunity to be candid. The superior should show from the outset that he will be candid. Hiding one's own views will only lead to a defeat of the implied contract – a meeting to improve performance. While a discussion of activities will usually arise in any analysis of performance, activities should never be allowed to become the focus of discussion. Never start a discussion of them or end with one.

It is not helpful, though it is comforting, to dwell on 'no

control' items. These are things which inhibit performance but which cannot be changed: 'If only we could get another girl.' 'If only the government regulation had not changed.'

A neat balance is required on the part of the superior between being participative and being rigid. If he is too participative the importance of formal review of performance will be lost. If he is too rigid, the commitment to higher performance, which may be generated, is lost instead.

Some superiors, with the best of intentions, give the impression that the major reward for high performance is that they will be pleased. It is no part of a subordinate's job to make a superior happy. It is his job to obtain output, not praise.

Salary discussion is usually avoided at the checkpoint meeting.

15.2.5 *The MOM – CPM cycle*
The managerial objectives meeting, checkpoint meeting cycle is usually something like that of Figure 33.

The first six steps are usually conducted annually and then the cycle repeats itself.

15.2.6 *Paperwork and records*
The effectiveness of MBO implementation is inversely proportional to the paperwork produced. The only document used to record the results of the managerial objectives meeting or the checkpoint meeting is the objective record sheet. This is fully described in Chapter 11. Only two typed copies are made. Objectives are a superior-manager contract. Extra copies will simply fill files and cause more work for the personnel department, but, worst of all, they weaken the impact of the contract. The superior's superior has no need of a copy, and it would reflect poor organisation and poor MBO implementation if he is sent one, as he has an objective record sheet from each of his own managers recording the managerial objectives meeting he himself has held.

It is practically always necessary for a manager to obtain staff assistance when he finally completes his objective record

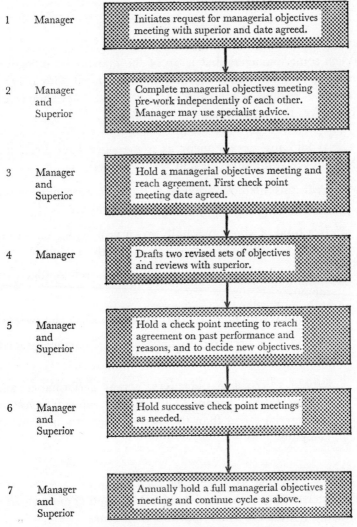

1	Manager	Initiates request for managerial objectives meeting with superior and date agreed.
2	Manager and Superior	Complete managerial objectives meeting pre-work independently of each other. Manager may use specialist advice.
3	Manager and Superior	Hold a managerial objectives meeting and reach agreement. First check point meeting date agreed.
4	Manager	Drafts two revised sets of objectives and reviews with superior.
5	Manager and Superior	Hold a check point meeting to reach agreement on past performance and reasons, and to decide new objectives.
6	Manager and Superior	Hold successive check point meetings as needed.
7	Manager and Superior	Annually hold a full managerial objectives meeting and continue cycle as above.

Figure 33   Managerial objectives meeting and checkpoint meeting cycle

sheets. He may have also obtained such assistance with his pre-work and if he wished, also have invited the staff man to the managerial objectives meeting.

15.2.7 *The value of the managerial objectives meeting*

When some managers first learn of the managerial objectives meeting they are not always fully in agreement with it for a variety of reasons, some valid and some not. They should ask themselves these questions:

Would my development as a manager have been improved if my superior had used this method?

Will this method provide a more comprehensive and effective method of coaching and appraisal?

Is a total of about two half days a year with each of my managers too much time to spend on this activity?

Would I like my superior to introduce this system with me now?

Would my own managers like me to introduce this system?

Would I be prepared to have my performance judged, after a trial, on such a system?

Would a record of objectives, actual performance and appraisal be a sounder way of conveying a sense of managerial talent than the method presently used in my company?

15.2.8 *A comparison with traditional appraisal*

To understand the managerial objectives meeting more clearly, compare it with the usual appraisal conference:

	Old	*New*
Time focus	Primarily past	Primarily future
Time taken	$\frac{1}{2}$ to 1 hour	4 to 8 hours
Role of superior	Judge	Counsellor

	Old	*New*
Role of manager	Judged	Initiator
Focus of evaluation	What went wrong last year – personality variables	What will go right next year – performance
Objective	Evaluation	Planning
Location of meeting	Superior's office	Manager's office
Emphasis on superior	None	How he can help his subordinate
Typical use	To reward, punish, and to some extent career plan	To motivate
Communication of appraisal	Sometimes not revealed to subordinate	Always revealed to subordinate

New concepts introduced – Chapter 15

CHECKPOINT MEETING (CPM):
> A superior-manager meeting, usually held quarterly, at which the manager's progress towards objectives is reviewed.

MANAGERIAL OBJECTIVES MEETING (MOM):
> A four- to eight-hour meeting between a manager and his superior to establish future objectives for the manager.

16 Corporate MBO Implementation

I once asked a farmer for directions to a neighbouring village and he told me 'you can't get there from here'. I sometimes run into the same problem with senior managers when discussing corporate strategy.

Some organisations have no philosophy and their style is essentially that of the bland leading the bland.

If a staff group initiates horizon decision studies then top management should get rid of their in-baskets.

Some firms observably go through a healthy 3–5 year 'identity moratorium' during which they decide not to decide what business they are in.

This chapter outlines the key elements of a corporate strategy and shows how objectives derived from it are linked with the managerial objectives established at team and pair meetings.

Not all companies have a clear corporate strategy and corporate plan but all should and can have one. To provide this the corporate objectives meeting was designed. It is one of the most powerful and necessary tools of Effective MBO. This three-day session provides an opportunity for a comprehensive review of the organisation's resources and alternatives and the meeting supplies the opportunity to decide what should be done about them.

Only after the top team has participated in the managerial objectives seminar, team objectives meeting and the managerial objectives meeting are they ready to start to develop a corporate strategy. It is best to improve the top team before it starts to improve the company.

This meeting is conducted only once per firm and it is solely for the top team. Each member of the top team completes about twenty hours of pre-work. The meeting is attended by the full top team and one or two outside consultants. The importance of the meeting, which is designed to tap all the resources of the top team, is indicated by the decisions made at it which affect all managers.

These include: philosophy of management, what business the company is in, optimal organisation chart, organisation development strategy, corporation-government relations, corporate five-year goals, career policy, product policy, top team members' responsibilities, liability-resource inventory, and management manpower inventory. The importance of these decisions varies with the organisation, as does the work already done on each. Through a variety of structured activities and measuring devices, these areas are held up for inspection, and plans are made to modify them if necessary.

Some of the key questions which arise are: Where is our organisation today? How has the environment changed? What can be done best? What business are we in? What business should we be in? How do we get there? Any top team has considered these questions previously. The corporate objectives meeting provides a longer period and a freer discussion climate in which to arrive at an optimum solution to which all will be committed.

At the meeting itself, these questions, based on pre-work, are answered.

16.1 Strategy questions

1 *Market developments*
Rank from 1 to 5 the five market developments which will most affect the company over the next ten years.

2 *Technological developments*
Rank from 1 to 5 the five technological developments which will most affect the company over the next ten years.

3 Competitive actions
Rank from 1 to 5 the five changes competitors are likely to make which will most affect the company over the next ten years.

4 Government actions
Rank from 1 to 5 the five government actions likely to be made which will most affect the company over the next ten years.

5 Optimum production facilities for the present
What should the optimum location, size and type of production facilities for the company be now?

6 Executive committee effectiveness areas
In what ten ways would the company be different in ten years' time if the executive committee were highly effective over the next few years.

7 Strengths and weaknesses
- (a) What are the three major strengths of the company now compared to its competitors?
- (b) What are the three major weaknesses of the company now compared to its competitors?

8 Critical areas
Suppose the company does not meet its return on investment, or other objectives, over the next five to ten years: agree on the ten reasons which would most probably explain it.

9 Past decisions
For the major decisions affecting the company over the last five years, agree which were:

- (a) Good decisions but should have been made earlier
- (b) Good decisions but implementation should have been delayed

(c) Good decisions and made at the right time
(d) Poor decisions in the light of subsequent events

10 *Actual past policies*
Compose short paragraphs stating clearly what the actual company policy has been for the past five years concerning: marketing, finance, manufacturing, procurement, personnel, research and development, product diversification, and acquisition.

11 *Acquisition policy*
Rank from 1 to 5 the five most important criteria by which an acquisition should be appraised.

12 *Business we are in*
Compose a short paragraph outlining each of the following:

(a) The business the company is in now
(b) The business the company could and should be in five years hence
(c) The business the company could and should be in ten years hence

13 *Product policy*
Agree on a desirable product mix, by sales percentage, for five and ten years' time.

14 *Proposed policies*
Compose short paragraphs stating clearly what is the best achievable policy for the next five years concerning marketing, finance, manufacturing, procurement, personnel, research and development, product diversification, and acquisition.

15 *Ten year Predictions*
Agree on the most probable figures for ten years hence

(a) Product line accounting for greatest £ profit

(b) Most profitable product line accounting for at least 10 per cent of profit

(c) Sales volume

(d) Sales distribution by geographic area

16 *Priorities for capital*

Rank capital priorities on the return on investment potential over five years. Also distribute 100 units of new money as it should be allocated over five years.

17 *Finance*

Identify the feasible major sources of financing and the approximate amounts you think obtainable for the next five years and the five years after that.

A corporate objectives meeting has a profound impact on the organisation because important changes usually follow it. An analysis of such changes has revealed that they are often ones that the executive had wished to make for some time but had neither opportunity nor time to tackle and think through to an agreed decision. This meeting frequently leads to the decision to establish a series of management project teams charged with casting optimum policies and procedures for the organisation.

The single most important output of the corporate objectives meeting is the beginning of a clear corporate strategy.

16.2 Corporate strategy

Company objectives must flow from corporate strategy. For instance a change in strategy concerning product mix will lead to a variety of changes in annual objectives concerning production facilities, sales, and capital requirements.

Strategy, in essence, defines the nature of the business and, in the broadest sense, how the business will operate. The nub strategy question is, 'What business are we to be in?' Another important question is, 'What do we want our competitive advantages to be?' Strategy is concerned with such things as the nature and rate of diversification or geographical expansion, the rate of new capital input, and the minimum anticipated return required on new capital projects. Other key decisions concern major budget allocations, such as the percentage to be spent on research and development, marketing or advertising, the brand, product, and customer mix policy, the rate of growth policy, and the market penetration policy.

Strategy is definitely not concerned with long-range projections of existing sales curves. This can be a useful exercise in statistical prediction, but it is not the same as establishing corporate strategy. 'Where do we expect to go?' is quite a different question from 'What do we want to be?'

Without a strategy each senior executive, and to a degree each manager, becomes involved in setting company policy. If this worked, there might be some good in it, but the thought of an eighty-man policy-making group is not attractive. Without a strategy, crisis management is a way of life. What might have had a preplanned response would get instead a reaction too rapid for things to be patched up. In-baskets usually are full and the 'coordinator' starts to appear with increasing frequency on the organisation chart. Files are full of alibi paper and heart attacks and ulcers are at a higher rate than normal.

16.2.1 *Some strategy statements are window dressing*

Some strategy statements are simply window dressing for external consumption. Such strategy statements as these are not a guide to action and are no aid in planning:

> To build public confidence and continuing friendly feeling for products and services bearing the Company's name and brands through sound, competitive advertising, promotion, selling, service, and personal contacts.

> To provide good jobs, wages, and working conditions, work satisfaction, and opportunities for advancement conducive to the most productive performance and also

the stablest possible employment, all in exchange for loyalty, initiative, skill, care, effort, attendance, and teamwork on the part of employees – the contributions of individual employees that result in 'value to the Company' and for which the employee is being paid.

To co-operate both with suppliers and with distributors, contractors, and others facilitating distribution, installation, and servicing of Company products so that Company efforts are constructively integrated with theirs for mutually effective public service and competitive, profitable progress.

To adapt Company policies, products, services, facilities, plans, and schedules to meet continuously, progressively, foresightedly, imaginatively, and voluntarily the social, civic, and economic responsibilities commensurate with the opportunities afforded by the size, success, and nature of the business and the public's confidence in it as a corporate enterprise.

. . . and after we have achieved all these we will ask the Lord to 'move over'.

Far more effective strategy statements might be:

To be a research-based company by spending at least 60 per cent more on R & D than the nearest competitor and at least 2·1 per cent of sales.

To be a quality order company by accepting no contracts under £200,000.

To be a flexible company by owning no single fixed asset valued above £50,000 and by having no leases of a term longer than five years.

Key elements of corporate strategy statements include the proportion of sales spent on specific functions or services. For example, should research and development expense be 0·5 per cent or 3·5 per cent? Should the company match its

226

competitors brand for brand and gimmick for gimmick or should it not? Until these strategy decisions are known the R & D manager or a brand manager cannot really do a satisfactory job in setting his objectives. Fortunately most strategy decisions as these tend to change very infrequently, and when they do change, all those concerned know about it very quickly.

16.2.2 *Linking strategy to managerial objectives*
Managerial objectives are not a reflection of 'doing your own thing'. In a well designed MBO installation the objectives of every manager link up clearly with the overall corporate plan

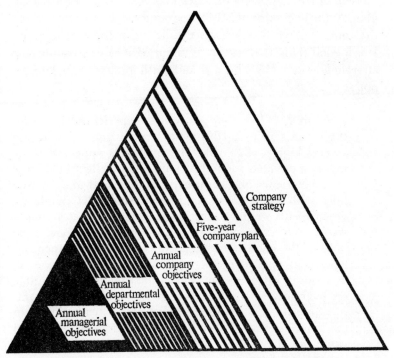

Figure 34   From company strategy to managerial
objectives

(*Managerial objectives are embedded in the company strategy and
five-year plan*)

which goes under many names, such as strategy, goals, five year objectives, and long range planning. The manager's objectives are an integral part of the whole.

The relationship of company strategy to managerial objectives can be seen as the sequence: company strategy, five-year company plan, annual company objectives, annual divisional/departmental objectives and then annual managerial objectives. This relationship is shown by Figure 34 which was drawn to illustrate that it is company strategy which sets the boundary of the firm and that the other four elements are subsequent derivatives of it.

Linking not automatic. The objectives of one manager must be related to the objectives of other managers and to an overall plan. At the beginning of MBO programmes it is often discovered that one manager's objectives conflict with those of another. It is a good thing to discover. Without MBO this cross purpose effort might not have been found until perhaps too late, or not at all.

> Prior to MBO one company had experienced losses for three years running during a growth period, following several high-profit years. The managers appeared to be highly motivated and industrious, had excellent functional area experience and knowledge, and desired to cooperate fully with each other. Analysis revealed that while all departments were working hard, they were all apparently working toward conflicting corporate objectives. The bulk of the engineering department's time was spent on maintenance, that of the marketing department was on new brand introduction, that of the executive committee on overseas expansion, while a key staff assistant was spending most of his time predicting political climate in the home country. Taken separately, these directions had value but they simply did not form an integrated set of linked objectives.

Some highly motivated managers set objectives to maximise the effectiveness of their own position but which if achieved may not lead to maximising the effectiveness of others, because the objectives simply do not link together. This condition is most often seen between such functions as sales and credit, research and production, and sometimes production and sales. MBO clarifies the need for linking objectives and thus provides a starting point for it.

The process of linking objectives. When a strategy exists MBO produces a formal system whereby objectives are linked. The timing, periodicity, time perspective and degree of involvement are a function of the technology and organisation structure.

Following is an example from Honeywell:

> The process begins each spring with a memorandum from the chairman setting forth some general goals of the corporation for the next three years, suggesting certain areas of interest, and indicating roughly the contributions the various divisions might be expected to make to attain these ends. On the basis of this document, the division managers prepare their own three-year plans in fairly great detail.
>
> Then, in the autumn, these same officials begin planning for the fiscal year that begins on 1st January. The managers within each division prepare a planning book the first chapter of which details specific goals for the division in terms of profits, volume, return on assets, and new products. Subsequent chapters of the book present specific goals for each of the division's major functional units, with cross references indicating how the goals of one function will support those of other functions. While the individual goals of each manager may not be included in the book, the division's goals are based upon those set by the managers.
>
> The work done in the spring to set forth a context within which detailed planning can take place provides the necessary direction from the top of the corporation. In the autumn, specific goals and objectives can be set at lower levels in the organisation with the expectation that they will mesh into the overall plan.

With relatively minor variations this procedure is widely used in Effective MBO implementations. The process followed is very similar to that of sound budget allocation and often is done with it. The important differences are that it is concerned with outputs (objectives) rather than inputs (budgets) and that the initial plan comes from the top down and is based on what the company wishes to achieve.

The down-up-down linking system. The down-up-down linking system is the name given to the procedure used in Effective MBO to get the best set of linked objectives for a company. In essence, it involves draft objectives being passed downward (the roll-down), a formal reaction to and revision of them from below, then being passed upward (the roll-up), and a final passing down of objectives on which all managerial objectives are based and to which they are linked. Without this full cycle installed in this way, MBO is not being fully utilised.

The steps are these:

1 At the beginning of the prior year top management reviews its strategy and plan and drafts a set of objectives for the coming period. (January–February)
2 These objectives are considered by the next lowest level and usually discussed with the level below that. Usually, fifty to seventy managers are involved at this stage. Revised objectives are developed. (March–April)
3 Top management considers these revised objectives and develops a final draft of objectives for the following period. (May–June)

The first one or two trials are often a little clumsy and much difficulty is experienced in tying all the sub-unit objectives to the company objectives. This usually leads, in turn, to a sharp increase in meetings, for the adjustment period only. What is happening at these meetings is the process of realistically linking objectives. The surface agenda may be 'You can't do that', 'It cannot work', 'How does that relate to our plans?' or 'Our objectives must have priority'; but beneath all of these is 'How can we get all our objectives linked together?' These discussions often uncover basic flaws in organisational design not previously identified – flaws which perhaps do not simply inhibit but actually prevent linking. During this adjustment period there needs to be available a mechanism, usually an external consultant, to identify such structural faults and bring them to the attention of management.

As the organisation gains experience with this process all managers tend to plan ahead so that they may have their own draft objectives prepared prior to receiving the draft from top management. This can be most important. A crucial part of this whole process is the reaction and sorting out that takes place when the top-down and bottom-up plans meet.

New concepts introduced – Chapter 16

CORPORATE OBJECTIVES MEETING (COM):
> A three-day meeting attended by the executive committee to develop long range objectives.

DOWN-UP-DOWN SYSTEM:
> An objective-setting process where draft objectives are first passed downward, then upward and then downward again.

ROLL-DOWN:
> Passing objectives downward.

ROLL-UP:
> Passing objectives upward.

17 The MBO Specialist

The MBO specialist is not responsible for implementing MBO; line management is.

The MBO specialist is first a change agent – not a writer.

Companies that propose to implement MBO usually appoint one or more internal MBO specialists who are assisted by an external MBO consultant. The appointment is usually for a specific term of two to four years. The man appointed obviously requires natural aptitude as an internal consultant and also special training. He should be able to:

Write effectiveness areas and effectiveness standards for any position

Write objectives for any position

Design a measuring system for any objective

Write a plan for any objective

Align effectiveness areas and effectiveness standards horizontally and vertically

Align objectives horizontally and vertically

Overcome resistance to change

Conduct one-day in-company sessions on:

The Company MBO programme

How to write effectiveness areas, effectiveness standards and objectives

How to conduct the managerial objectives meeting and checkpoint meetings

Conduct the managerial objectives seminar

Conduct the team objectives meeting

Consult at or prior to managerial objectives meeting

These skills are in effect the behavioural objectives of the MBO specialist's course.

MBO advisers need to have a considerable amount of training and a broad view of their jobs but still need outside support. As one adviser wrote:

> Although the basic principles of MBO are relatively simple and can be readily assimilated without extensive training in management techniques, we were undoubtedly right in deciding to bring in mangement consultants at the outset. Without this professional boost, I am firmly convinced that the project would not have got off the ground.

They also need to learn to become professional in attitude and to keep their own needs in check.

> Undoubtedly the most difficult task of the specialist is to remain on the 'outside'. While the aim is to be nothing more than a catalyst, there have been times when the attitudes and abilities of individuals have been such that one has the greatest difficulty in avoiding the executive role.

17.1 The six-week MBO specialist course

MBO specialists can be trained in about six weeks. At the end of that time they can start immediately to introduce MBO under supervision. Two of the weeks are full time study, and four are practical application in an ongoing MBO installation.

The course programme is:

Thirty hours of pre-reading and pre-work

Writing effectiveness areas and effectiveness standards for ten hypothetical positions

Writing effectiveness areas and effectiveness standards for five live positions

Learning the major MBO systems

Learning change facilitation techniques

Learning how to implement MBO on a company-wide basis

Participating in two managerial objectives seminars

Learning effective MBO start-up procedures

Participating in two team objectives meetings

Observing four managerial objectives meetings

From the objectives, and the programme of the MBO specialist's course his role should be clearer.

With the assistance of the external MBO consultant as required, the MBO specialist's job is to conduct the various instrumented meetings on request. After the team objectives meeting he helps the team draft job and unit effectiveness descriptions. After the managerial objectives meeting he helps each manager draft his objectives and plan and advises on how best to link such plans with those of others. After the corporate objectives meeting he assists the top team in preparing a formal long range planning document.

17.2 Common errors of MBO specialists

The most common errors of an MBO specialist are:

To think he has the responsibility to install MBO

To do the things that a line manager should do concerning MBO

To identify unduly with one of top, middle or lower management

To spend more than 5 per cent of his time in his office

To keep files or to have a desk

To use his office as a storehouse for forms

To believe a managerial objectives meeting is some kind of verbal wrestling match at which he is a referee somewhat on the superior's side

To give priority to his needs to get a job done rather than to the manager's need to understand what is being done

To use a steamroller approach to deal with resistance or to hope that line management will do so

To fail to accept resistance as legitimate

17.2.1 *The specialist who does too much*

Some MBO specialists work in such a way as to remove initiative from the line as this in-company manual shows:

> We (the MBO specialists) start the ball rolling by briefing ourselves thoroughly regarding the key objectives and key result areas that are likely to apply in the particular unit and to be thought important by its top management. We achieve this by holding a series of three or four meetings with the head of the unit and one or two of his senior staff if he wishes to invite them. In order to be prepared for these initial meetings we have in fact armed ourselves with lists of typical key areas, some or all of which are likely to interest the managers of different kinds of units.
>
> These talks with the head of the unit take place over three or four weeks, and during this time the specialists are busy familiarising themselves with the work of the unit. In a factory they will be working with foremen, superintendents, and the accountant, looking primarily at control information, searching for the measurements they know they will need in helping managers to specify results, to set their targets. This is a vital phase of our work. We must get to know the realities of what goes on

– the real strengths and weaknesses – if we are to avoid superficiality.

And from another description showing inappropriate hyperactivity:

> Those agreed will be collected together from this and other sets of objectives by the MBO specialist, who will analyse them and refer them to the overall unit manager for consideration, and possibly for inclusion in the unit objectives plan.

This could not be designed better to build a resistance and reduce commitment. Compare the description above with the process of the team objectives meeting which puts the team, not the specialist, in the driver's seat.

17.3 The position of the MBO specialist

The most important questions raised about the position are:

> Within or outside personnel?
> Within or outside training?
> How close to the top?
> Inside or outside the firm?
> Has he line responsibility?
> Is he basically in a staff career route?
> Does he report to an individual or to a committee?

The Effective MBO method places the position outside personnel and training. The specialist reports to the MBO committee.

17.4 The MBO committee

All Effective MBO implementations make use of an MBO committee. If the MBO implementation is linked with a broader programme of organisational change, this committee is usually called the 'organisational effectiveness committee'. It has the responsibility for MBO implementation and reports to the executive committee. MBO specialists report to it or are members of it, if there are not too many of them, in which case they form an MBO team.

The committee is chaired by a member of the executive committee and one or two others of the executive committee are members. The chairmanship rotates annually. Two line managers are also members and appropriate staff personnel.

Clearly this committee is dominated by the line. It must be if the line is to take responsibility for MBO implementation. The staff certainly cannot take it. A mix of functions is also important. The external MBO consultant advises the committee.

The MBO specialist is given, and assumes, no responsibility for implementing MBO. This responsibility stays firmly with the line.

17.5 Period in position

While the position of MBO specialist could be a worthwhile career for many, MBO is still too young for us to see any clear career trends. It is not desirable, however, to have anyone in the position full time for less than two years, while using part-time appointments simply means that no decision has been made. A bright manager with the correct attitude toward internal consultancy can learn the job in about two months, with most of this being working time. Many see the drafting of effectiveness areas as the MBO specialist's major job but it is not that at all. He is really a change agent. His major skill is in sensing the real reasons for resistance and knowing how to resolve them. He must learn to be sensitive to the organisation and to the people in it. Most important, he must come to know by direct experience the effects of his interventions. This experience will be acquired only after many months on the job and with an expert's advice.

237

MBO COMMITTEE:

A group of managers and others who have the responsibility for Effective MBO implementation.

MBO CONSULTANT (MC):

A person trained in MBO who works from outside the company.

MBO SPECIALIST (MS):

A person trained in MBO who works full time for the company.

MBO SPECIALIST COURSE:

A four week training programme for those wishing to become MBO specialists.

MBO TEAM:

A group of MBO specialists and consultants within a particular company.

18 Effective MBO Start-up

The way MBO is started allows a fairly accurate prediction of how it will end.

Much resistance arises simply because top management is clearly doing the wrong thing.

Commitment is never obtained by pseudo-participative means.

Crash programmes to introduce MBO usually fail.

Always start MBO at the top.

The way MBO is started allows a fairly accurate prediction of how it will end. If, from the start, commitment is sought and obtained, most implementation problems can be overcome.

Effective MBO accepts the premise that commitment has to be earned and that this can be done only with intelligence and honesty. Intelligence is needed simply to avoid taking inappropriate action. Much resistance arises in organisations simply because top management is clearly doing the wrong thing. Honesty is also needed – about objectives, methods, and techniques. Without it there will be low trust, and with low trust, change is usually unnecessarily painful for all concerned.

Commitment is never obtained by pseudo-participative means. Effective MBO does not allow such manipulation, and its instrumentation and other devices effectively prevent it. Middle management must not be asked if they agree to an MBO scheme if they cannot say no. A manager must not be asked for his opinion if his superior's mind is made up. Only by honesty is commitment obtained.

The six steps for the start of an MBO programme are:

> Managers learn what MBO means
> Survey of existing conditions is made
> Three-level meeting is conducted

Objective of programme is established
Implementation method is established
Top team start

18.1 Managers learn what MBO means

A characteristic start in MBO is for five to ten senior managers
to read a book like this one or preferably to take a course in
MBO such as the managerial objectives seminar. It is best if
two or more of the top team are among them. It is also desirable
if those known not to be too enthused about management
training be encouraged to attend. After their attendance these
managers fairly accurately judge the probable usefulness of
MBO to their organisation.

After their return from the seminar – they may have attended
different ones – these managers meet together. The object
of this meeting is to decide whether or not they would recommend to the executive committee to proceed further. If they
decide to so recommend, and their recommendation is accepted
by the board, a sound next step is a formal MBO survey to
determine existing conditions.

18.2 MBO survey

It is helpful to precede an MBO implementation decision with
a survey. The survey provides a mild unfreezing effect, offers
information for consultants and top management, and is a
reference point against which to measure change. This survey
is best conducted by outside consultants who are seen as
impartial, have done it before and have comparative results
available. The usual sample is the top two to three levels.

The survey should look at four things:

Effectiveness areas
Superior-subordinate relations

18.2.1 *Effectiveness areas survey*

An effectiveness areas survey reviews all key effectiveness areas seen to be part of particular positions. Which position for instance is responsible for pricing? Which for return on new capital projects? And so on. The survey results are produced on a large wall chart with a paper copy for the executive committee. It looks something like Figure 35. If the survey is comprehensive the chart might be as big as 3 ft by 15 ft.

The usual findings of such a survey show that a high degree of overlap exists in many effectiveness areas and that some areas are not covered at all. This part of the survey is based on the assumption that the authority and responsibility for an effectiveness area must be centered on a single position.

18.2.2 *Superior-subordinate relations survey*

A superior-subordinate relations survey would provide a comprehensive appraisal of inter-level relationships. Such questions as these are included:

> How often in the past year has your superior let you know how you are doing?
> Do you know what you are expected to achieve?
> Do you know your unit's role in the organisation?

This kind of survey is particularly useful to repeat annually after the programme has begun. It acts as a fairly scientific appraisal of how well the organisation is moving toward MBO.

18.2.3 *Problem areas survey*

The problem area survey is less structured than the other parts and consists essentially of answers to the question, 'How could things be improved?' This method of wording, by the way, is much better than 'What is wrong around here?' Empirical tests have shown that the first way of asking it produces a more thoughtful, accurate and useful response.

Position Area	Managing Director	Director—Marketing	Director—Production	Director—Industrial Relations	Director—Finance	Purchasing	R & D	Personnel
Accounts Receivable								
Return on Investment								
Inventory								
Delivery								
Quality								
New products								

Figure 35   Effectiveness area survey chart

(If two people are responsible for the same thing, one of them

In addition to focusing in turn on the functional areas and their subparts, the survey also investigates such things as:

Information flow	Decision-making quality
Role clarity	Innovation rate
Participation	Staff role clarity
Delegation	Policies
Structure	Procedures

This kind of survey also provides a valuable diagnosis which any organisation would want to make periodically.

18.2.4 *Organisation health survey*

PRODUCTIVITY:
The degree to which the organisation is seen as placing a high value on productivity.

LEADERSHIP:
The degree to which the organisation is seen as having effective leadership.

ORGANISATION STRUCTURE:
The degree to which the organisation structure is seen as appropriate.

COMMUNICATION:
The degree to which the organisation is seen as having open communication.

CONFLICT MANAGEMENT:
The degree to which disagreement is seen to occur when necessary and to be used productively.

HUMAN RESOURCE MANAGEMENT:
The degree to which the organisation's human resources are seen to be well utilised.

PARTICIPATION:
The degree to which participation is seen to be used.

CREATIVITY:
The degree to which the organisation is seen as creative.

Figure 36   Organisation health survey measures

(*These eight scales provide an accurate picture of how the organisation is seen*)

A survey of organisation health is designed to discover attitudes of managers to the organisation. The most important areas to survey include attitudes to productivity, leadership, organisation structure, communication, conflict management, human resource management, participation, and creativity.

Eight such scales are defined in Figure 36 and illustrative questions are shown in Figure 37.

The results of the survey are first discussed with the top team. After this discussion the top team is asked whether it wishes to proceed to the next step, the three level meeting.

		Agree	Disagree
69	People don't try to 'win' arguments here, instead they work for the best solution.		
70	There is a great opportunity for advancement in this organisation.		
71	Many decisions are postponed if everyone concerned does not at first agree.		
72	My own ideas for change are given a good hearing.		
73	Very little time is wasted here.		
74	Our managers know what they are doing.		
75	I know how this organisation operates.		

Figure 37   Illustrative questions—organisation
health survey

(*Eighty such questions cover all that an organisation could be*)

18.3 Three-level meeting

A crucial step in an MBO start-up is a meeting of the top three levels, of about 25–45 managers. The meeting usually lasts a full day. The participants in this meeting include the top man, be he chairman or general manager, all his subordinates who compose the second level and most of their subordinates who compose the third level.

The objective of the meeting is for the group, as a whole, to come to one of three decisions concerning MBO:

> Proceed
> Postpone the decision to proceed
> Do not proceed

It is helpful to use an outside consultant to ensure that the meeting does not simply decide to proceed, or not, without giving the matter full consideration.

Inputs to the meeting, which may have been distributed in advance, are the reports of the managers who attended an outside course such as the managerial objectives seminar and also the results of the MBO survey.

The meeting starts with an exposition of what MBO is, followed by a question and answer period. This kind of start-up initiates the rule of Effective MBO, which is that decisions to implement MBO programmes should not be made at the executive committee level alone but should involve the whole of the next level in a real sense, and should be made only after some knowledge has been acquired. This is followed by an explanation of the remainder of the day which poses three questions to teams of five to six managers. The three questions are:

1 Why might MBO not work in this company?
2 What must be decided or solved if MBO is to be properly implemented?
3 Is it likely that the MBO programme will succeed and what is your recommendation concerning it?

Each team reports back through a single spokesman to the whole group after the discussion of each question.

The first question may seem a negative way to start but the issues that are aired need to be aired if MBO is to succeed. This question is obviously the best way to get them out. Typical responses to the first question include:

18.3.1 *Replies to 'why might MBO not work in this company?'*

Resistance to change

Each man's responsibility is not specified clearly enough

Side issues (mostly union) take a good part of our time

Strength of opinion of some senior managers

Format and philosophy cuts across current and traditional procedures

Education time is lacking for both superiors and subordinates

Constant change in personnel

Inflexibility in assigning or obtaining resources

Tried in associated company and adverse comments spread by victims

Because of the many changes taking place in our company at this time

Management by crisis still exists in our organisation and an MBO plan would be sidetracked

Long history of independence of research scientists

Punishment and reward system does not exist

MBO requires planning and managers generally don't like to plan

MBO requires honesty and openness between superior and subordinate

Naturally the answers to this question initiate a discussion. To get all these points aired, and some resolved, early in the programme is better than letting such ideas drag along for several years. The mere process of asking such a question of course puts the executive committee in a good light. They are obviously willing to look at negative data. The three-level meeting is not a whitewash job on either side.

18.3.2. *Second-generation start-ups*

It is becoming increasingly common for companies to make a second attempt at putting in MBO, the so called 'second-generation' start-up. Naturally this is a ticklish business for a

246

great variety of reasons – not the least of which are the feelings involved. When such start-ups are faced honestly, however, and the reasons for prior lack of progress are fully aired, success is virtually assured. Such start-ups should always be initiated with a top-three or even top-four level meeting, then lasting two days.

18.4 Objectives of programme

If the three-level meeting decides to proceed with MBO the MBO committee is appointed. Its first jobs are to specify the objectives of the programme and to secure adequate implementation assistance.

One might think that the objective of an MBO programme would be simply 'to implement MBO'. An objective worded this way of course does not meet too many of the criteria of a good objective, especially specificity. The committee need to look at all of these elements of MBO and to agree which, usually all, they wish to obtain, in what time and for what level:

> Concept of effectiveness central in organisation
> Effectiveness areas established for units and positions
> Effectiveness standards established for units and positions
> Objectives established for units and positions
> Measurement methods established for units and positions
> Managers establish a plan to meet each objective
> Objectives linked horizontally
> Objectives linked vertically
> Objectives tied to a corporate plan
> MBO linked to budgeting system
> MBO linked to appraisal system

As MBO is a catalyst for many necessary changes, it is appropriate for objectives to be established in non-MBO areas. Typical of these might be: move decision levels downward, introduce participative management, increase organisational flexibility, remove management layer, facilitate a merger, build executive teams or introduce marketing orientation.

When objectives are clearly established the MBO committee turns to implementation.

18.5 Implementation method established

One of the crucial aspects of MBO implementation is timing.

Per manager time over three years:
(Assuming 1 superior and 5 subordinates)

Managerial Objectives Seminar	5
Team Objectives Meeting (as subordinate)	3
Team Objectives Meeting (as superior)	3
Managerial Objectives Meeting (as subordinate)	$\frac{1}{2}$
Managerial Objectives Meeting (with each subordinate)	$2\frac{1}{2}$
Pre-work time	4
	18 days

The time involved for a manager in a full-scale MBO programme is about eighteen days over a period of three years, or six days a year. With Effective MBO the manager attends the managerial objectives seminar for five days, two team objectives meetings for three days each – first as a subordinate and then as a superior, a managerial objectives meeting as a subordinate and then perhaps five of the same as a superior for a total of another three days, while other activities, together with pre-work, average out to about four days. None of this is training downtime. The first five days focus directly on improving the manager's effectiveness, whereas all other stages are highly task-orientated job-related meetings designed to produce immediate changes.

The overall time taken to complete a total programme is usually about two to three years. If all four instrumented stages are used, some parts of the organisation will have completed stages one to three within the first six months, while other parts of the organisation will have hardly started stage one. This has many beneficial effects. MBO programmes need to be flexible so that organisational sub-parts move at a comfortable rate of change for them, and the internal trainers get a rapid exposure to all stages so that they are better prepared for widespread implementation later.

The total consultant time, as a rough average, is six to nine days per manager over three years or two to three days per year per manager. How this is split between inside and outside consultants depends on the skill of those available internally, the company size, the speed required, the degree of resistance and the complexity of the company's MBO-associated problems.

18.5.1. *Avoid crash programmes*

Crash programmes to introduce MBO usually fail. A paperwork overlay may result, but certainly not commitment to what is printed. For this reason the introduction of MBO, while it must be well planned, should not be tightly scheduled. Not all managers in a division should, or need to, use it within a month or two of each other. Individual response to change varies. Some otherwise willing managers may want to wait a few months before holding a managerial objectives meeting, while many will want one immediately. A particular manager may wish to see what happens to his golfing partner in another division before participating himself.

18.5.2 *Discussion of implementation of MBO*

A fully participative discussion of implementation is essential to MBO. Resistance to change is reduced if there can be agreement on the rate and method of implementation. It is as effective to have discussions on the way a change is to be introduced as it is to discuss the nature of the change itself. Such discussions will cover what the first steps should be, what the rate of change should be, what the appropriate sequence of changes should be, and who should be involved in what elements of the implementation. When this method is used successfully, it sometimes happens that the unit undergoing the change says to management, 'Leave us alone. Come back in two weeks or two months and the changes will be in.' A wise manager accepts that kind of offer.

It is clear that if commitment is wanted a necessary condition is to design a clear programme but also to pace the introduction as flexibly as possible so as to both recognise and accept individual differences.

18.6 Top team first

The top team will have gone a long way with MBO in the first year. It is important that they do so. Their participation will have certainly led to many changes being made.

Also within a year the so-called 2 to 3 level objectives meetings are started between those who report to the top man and their subordinates. This starts MBO and change moving through the organisation.

New concepts introduced – Chapter 18

MBO SURVEY:
   A survey undertaken as part of MBO start-up to determine existing conditions in the firm.

SECOND GENERATION START-UP:
   A second attempt at MBO implementation.

The process between the time when a company first thinks seriously about MBO and the time when it commits major resources to implementing it.

19 The Benefits of Effective MBO

MBO strengthens the superior-subordinate relationship.

A major benefit of MBO is to aid a company to achieve its image of potential.

MBO has passed the test of profit improvement.

When MBO is implemented by those with experience, its main benefit is as a change catalyst.

One of the reasons for the popularity of MBO is that it has a wide range of benefits. There are clear benefits to the subordinate, to the superior and to the organisation as a whole.

19.1 MBO benefits the subordinate

MBO is directly beneficial to subordinates. In summary, with MBO, subordinates have the following advantages:

Subordinates benefits
Knowledge of what is expected of them
Performance measurement
Clarified authority and responsibility
Increased job satisfaction

MBO provides what is essentially a contract between a superior-subordinate pair. As a minimum the contract states what both parties feel is an appropriate level of performance. With this kind of contract the possibility of the excuse 'You didn't tell me I was supposed to . . .' vanishes. The subordinate's objectives are clearly laid out. He knows what is expected of him. Because of this the subordinate can get on with the job to be done. He is relieved of any ambiguity about what he is to accomplish.

MBO not only provides a clear charter of what is to be achieved, it can and should also provide a clear measurement device by which the achievement can be measured. Psychologists have demonstrated repeatedly that performance improves if measurement data on the performance are made available. Any manager is helped a great deal if he knows whether or not he is performing successfully.

As objectives are set, it very often becomes clear that while a manager is held responsible, he has no authority. A conversation like this will frequently occur:

Superior: 'Yes, I agree you are responsible for achieving that objective.'

Manager: 'I accept that I am, but you are now making the key decisions concerning it.'

Superior: 'Well, we had better decide either that I accept the responsibility or that you make the decisions.'

Manager: 'All right. On what basis should we make the decision?'

This simple conversation is likely to be repeated at all levels in an organisation. It will arise most often in the one-over-one situation where a single manager reports to another. This type of structure can work, but responsibilities have to be sharply defined, as overlap can easily occur.

Most men and women enjoy work as well as play. What they don't enjoy is being hindered when doing either. One thing that makes organised games fun is that effectiveness standards, objectives, measurement methods, roles, authority and responsibilities are clearly defined. They are learned as a child and crystal clear to all concerned. Those who do not want organisations to be clearly structured should consider the degree of structure in games and the enjoyment we have when playing them. Most dissatisfaction in organisations stems from a lack of clarity concerning such things as authority and from fuzzy performance standards, not from the simple existence or absence of them. MBO can help clear things up and make work more enjoyable.

Quite apart from monetary rewards, most of us find intrinsic enjoyment in a job well done. If we did not, we would not spend so much time building and sailing our boats, growing our roses, or processing our films. An important reward that we seek in these and other activities is the knowledge that we have performed well. This is true also in most kinds of managerial work, and this intrinsic reward must be recognised and understood when motivation to work is being considered. However, concrete rewards are also usually enjoyed by all of us. These may relate to promotion, to still more interesting work, increased responsibility, or more salary.

These direct quotations from managers involved in MBO, reported by Tosi, show the degree and variety of benefits MBO can generate:

> 'There is a kind of discipline involved in this programme. I had to sit down and think about what I am going to be doing next year. I need to spell out what kind of resources are required and when I expect a particular project to be accomplished.'

> 'While I did not have much to say in what the final determination of my goals were, at least I knew what my boss wanted and I knew what to do. I think this motivated me to work harder, or at least to work on those things that I knew were important to him. I also knew whether or not I achieved targets set for me.'

> '. . . a fantastic idea to have a voice along with your boss in setting individual goals. I thought it was a psychological lift. I think the chance to sit down with your boss is important.'

> 'I am now judged by my job performance and not by the way I comb my hair.'

A district engineer reported that the introduction of MBO in his district assisted him in these ways:

1 Determining and clarifying the important areas of the job without at the same time getting deeply involved in technical aspects.
2 The active participation of higher management in setting objectives within the framework of the Board's overall objectives.
3 The establishment of short- and long-term plans.
4 The introduction of a new organisation, details of which he had in mind for two years or so.
5 Improvement in lateral communication and the identification of practical operating problems, thereby leading to improved managerial performance.
6 The existence of a plan was itself a stimulus and provided the necessary motivation to get on with the job. A further stimulus arose from the fact that other levels of management were involved and all arrows were pointing in the same direction.
7 An all-round improvement in morale, relationships, and communications.

19.2 MBO benefits the superior

MBO is as directly useful to superiors as it is to subordinates. All of the five benefits for subordinates naturally benefit superiors as well. In addition, however, MBO provides four special benefits to superiors:

Superior benefits

MBO
Motivates subordinates
Strengthens relationships
Provides coaching framework
Eliminates weak appraisal methods

MBO motivates subordinates to higher performance. It does this because through it subordinates participate in the formulation of their own objectives, they help to decide how their own achievement of the objectives will be measured, and they have an opportunity to structure their job so that achievement is more likely. Obviously all of this must lead naturally to increased commitment and motivation. In other words, MBO leads to the manager being motivated by the job itself rather than solely by the hope of reward, or the personality and techniques used by his superior.

MBO always strengthens the superior-subordinate relationship. The pair now have a common task in setting objectives for a position with which both are involved. They both talk about work, roles, blockages and effectiveness far more than they did before. Some MBO programmes start with a four-hour meeting between the two parties in which to have an open discussion of all of these issues. This is often the first time they have done it.

MBO, if properly handled by the superior, can lead to a coaching relationship with his subordinate. Instead of acting as a source of orders, evaluative statements, and rewards and punishments, he helps his subordinate to achieve what both have agreed is desirable. The interaction changes from 'This is what I want you to do' to, 'How can I help you achieve your objectives?' This is not pie in the sky; it is a natural consequence of a properly designed and introduced MBO programme.

One of the biggest blockages between superiors and subordinates is often concerned with the appraisal method used. The worst method of appraisal, still widely used, is based on personality traits such as neatness, punctuality, diligence, and industry. Most subordinates find such appraisals insulting, and, in any case, they are of little value in assessing effectiveness or improving it. Industrial studies have discovered that telling a subordinate about personality faults is a sure way to inhibit any change in them. Most of us know very well what kind of people we are. Our wives and children tell us. We know we have faults and we try to work from our strengths. We want our superior to talk to us about performance not personality. We will draw our own inferences about our personality. This is what MBO provides.

Because of all of the above, although it is not always so described, MBO is a major management development method.

19.3 MBO benefits the organisation

MBO has been applied successfully to profit-making organisations of most types, to plants, to administrative organisations such as the public service, to educational organisations including universities, to military organisations at national and unit level, and to service organisations including hospitals and consulting firms.

Naturally, if MBO benefits managers as both superiors and subordinates, it must also benefit the organisation. There are some benefits, however, that apply primarily to the organisation as a whole:

Organisation Benefits

MBO
Induces managerial effectiveness as a central value
Focuses managerial effort
Facilitates co-ordinated effort
Provides profit potential
Provides objective reward criteria
Identifies advancement potential
Identifies development needs
Facilitates change

The underlying value in MBO is that of managerial effectiveness. To implement MBO is as if to say that managerial effectiveness is the central issue in the organisation. This idea alone can condition an organisation to make much better decisions concerning individuals and plans. The questions are always essentially the same:

> Is he effective?
> What must we do now to become effective?
> Will this result in improved effectiveness?
> How can I increase your effectiveness?

These are far more powerful questions than:

> What will he think of this?
> How did we do it last time?
> Would they mind if we did it this way?

MBO serves to focus managerial effort. The question raised insistently by MBO is, 'What does it take to be effective here?' Any manager who has a set of objectives will stop doing some things he need not do and will concentrate on what he needs to do to achieve his objectives. His effort is focused by his objectives.

MBO cannot succeed in a true sense unless the departments and the divisions in a firm act in co-ordination. MBO serves to identify unco-ordinated actions and to correct them.

MBO has a high profit potential. If it did not, there would be little point in getting excited about it. The profit comes as a result of the many benefits outlined here. Its main contribution to profit, though, comes from the emphasis it puts on managerial effectiveness and on sound integrated planning, rational execution and effective review.

One electrical utility reported these results from using MBO:

> The number of employees has been reduced from a peak of 4,800 at the end of 1965 to 3,700 at the present time – a reduction of 23 per cent with a slightly increased task.

> Stocks have been reduced by 50 per cent over the past four years.

System outages in terms of consumer hours lost/consumer have been reduced from about 120 minutes in 1960/61 to about 60 minutes in 1967/68.

MBO provides a sound method of appraising management performance. A central feature of MBO is a clear method of performance measurement which both superior and subordinate agree is as objective and accurate as possible. With good measurement, a better system of rewards for good performance is possible. It is a fatal mistake to overemphasise appraisal early in MBO implementation before managers really feel they know what they are doing. At the same time, not to associate MBO eventually with a reward system is another mistake. Some organisations, particularly the public service, do not emphasise monetary reward for merit in the short run. However, in the long run such reward is apparent in rapid promotions, so that one sees men in the most senior executive positions who have not reached forty.

In one very successful 5,000 member firm in Australia the performance of each of the top 300 managers is reviewed annually by the general manager. For each of the managers the general manager has a note from the manager's immediate superior which outlines the degree to which his objectives were achieved and gives a very short paragraph on the manager's advancement potential. With each division manager the general manager goes over the past five years' records of every manager. It takes only minutes per manager to do this. All managers know it is happening and all division managers know that their own work is being reviewed in the same way at board level. This is clearly a successful implementation of MBO with a strong emphasis on identifying, and advancing the 'fliers'.

While MBO can be used to facilitate advancement, it is also very useful to identify development needs. Some managers in a particular position may seriously under-perform. Without MBO this could go unrecognised. With MBO the reasons for

259

under-performance can usually be identified. The question is asked, 'What did this manager do or not do that contributed to his not meeting his objectives?' The answer may be poor planning skills, low motivation, or poor job knowledge. Whatever it is, a development programme can be designed to correct it if such a plan appears feasible. It often occurs that a manager is simply in the wrong job. This is most easily identified when high performance gives way to low.

When MBO is implemented by those with experience, its main benefit is as a change catalyst. It is a common occurrence for a well-implemented MBO system to lead to widespread reorganisation, a revised 'nature of business' policy, or even the removal of a layer of managers.

19.4 Overall benefits

MBO has some overall benefits which also recommend its use:

MBO, while not obviously theoretical, is based on many sound organisational and psychological principles. These include the focus on outputs of positions, feedback on performance, and the commitment arising from involvement.

MBO can be used in all parts of the organisation. It is true that it is easier to find measurements in manufacturing than in some service functions but the basic ideas can be applied everywhere.

MBO is flexible in the nature and degree of its implementation. It is not a go-no-go proposition. It is not 'this way or not at all'. To some extent MBO can be tailored to the style of the top manager in the organisation and to the readiness of the organisation to accept it.

MBO is not so complex a system that management needs to rely heavily on outside help to implement it. The ideas behind MBO are perfectly clear and the degree of success of its implementation will be equally clear.

While MBO is easily understood and is under the control of management, external assistance is undoubtedly useful. The external assistance is most often involved with setting of objectives for the top team, with decreasing resistance to change in the organisation, and with training internal consultants.

MBO is now fully tested. It is beyond its trial period and has passed the test of profit improvement.

Appendix A
Effective MBO Dictionary

ACTIVITY:
A particular thing a manager actually does or intends to do (Chapter 9).

ACTIVITY NETWORK:
A diagram of a particular combination of activities connected by arrows to show their sequential relationships (Chapter 9).

ACTIVITY SCHEDULE:
A visual arrangement of activities over a time period (Chapter 9).

ANOTHER'S AREA:
An effectiveness area a manager shows as his own which is really that of another manager (Chapter 6).

APPARENT EFFECTIVENESS:
The extent to which a manager gives the appearance of being effective (Chapter 1).

AREAS ALIGNMENT:
When effectiveness areas for a set of related positions have no overlap or underlap (Chapter 7).

CEA:
See Common Effectiveness Areas.

CHECKPOINT MEETING (CPM):
A superior-manager meeting, usually held quarterly, at which the manager's progress towards objectives is reviewed (Chapter 15).

COM:
See Corporate Objectives Meeting.

COMMON EFFECTIVENESS AREAS (CEA):
> Those effectiveness areas which may be and usually are associated with all managerial positions (Chapter 4).

CONVENTIONAL JOB DESCRIPTION:
> A written statement emphasising the input requirements of a particular managerial position (Chapter 1).

CORPORATE OBJECTIVES MEETING (COM):
> A three-day meeting attended by the executive committee to develop long range objectives (Chapter 16).

CO-WORKER:
> A person with whom a manager works who is neither his superior nor a subordinate (Chapter 12).

CO-WORKER EFFECTIVENESS AREA:
> A common effectiveness area concerned with the effectiveness of a manager's co-workers (Chapter 4).

CPM:
> See Checkpoint Meeting.

DEVELOPMENT EFFECTIVENESS AREA:
> A common effectiveness area concerned with a manager's preparation to meet his objectives (Chapter 4).

DOWN-UP-DOWN SYSTEM:
> An objective-setting process where draft objectives are first passed downward, then upward and then downward again (Chapter 16).

E:
> See Managerial Effectiveness.

EA:
> See Effectiveness Areas.

EFFECTIVENESS AREAS (EA):
> General output requirements of a managerial position (Chapter 3).

EFFECTIVENESS STANDARDS (ES):

Specific output requirements and measurement criteria of a managerial position (Chapter 3).

ES:

See Effectiveness Standards.

HORIZONTAL ALIGNMENT:

When the manager's effectiveness areas and objectives mesh well with those of other managers at his level (Chapter 7).

INNOVATIVE EFFECTIVENESS AREA:

A common effectiveness area concerned with a manager's innovations (Chapter 4).

INPUT AREA:

An incorrect statement of an effectiveness area which is based on an activity rather than a result (Chapter 6).

INPUTS:

What a manager does, or is to do, rather than what a manager achieves by doing it (Chapter 6).

INSTRUMENTATION:

A training method which minimises the instructor's role by the use of pre-work, task assignments and self-generated performance feedback (Chapter 12).

JED:

See Job Effectiveness Description.

JOB EFFECTIVENESS DESCRIPTION (JED):

A written statement specifying the effectiveness areas, effectiveness standards and authority of a particular managerial position (Chapter 1).

MANAGEMENT BY OBJECTIVES (MBO):

The establishment of effectiveness areas and effectiveness standards for managerial positions and the periodic conversion of these into measurable, time-bounded objectives linked vertically and horizontally and with future planning (Chapter 2).

MANAGER:
A person occupying a position in a formal organisation who is responsible for the work of at least one other person and who has formal authority over that person (Chapter 12).

MANAGER EFFECTIVENESS AREAS:
The effectiveness areas of a particular managerial position considered alone; they do not include the effectiveness areas of subordinates (Chapter 7).

MANAGERIAL EFFECTIVENESS (E):
The extent to which a manager achieves the output requirements of his position (Chapter 1).

MANAGERIAL OBJECTIVES MEETING (MOM):
A four- to eight-hour meeting between a manager and his superior to establish future objectives for the manager (Chapter 15).

MANAGERIAL OBJECTIVES SEMINAR (MOS):
A seminar conducted in-company or publicly where managers without line relationships to each other learn Effective MBO (Chapter 13).

MBO:
See Management by Objectives.

MBO COMMITTEE:
A group of managers and others who have the responsibility for Effective MBO implementation (Chapter 17).

MBO CONSULTANT (MC):
A person trained in MBO who works from outside the company (Chapter 17).

MBO SPECIALIST (MS):
A person trained in MBO who works full time for the company (Chapter 17).

MBO SPECIALIST COURSE:

A four week training programme for those wishing to become MBO specialists (Chapter 17).

MBO SURVEY:

A survey undertaken as part of MBO start-up to determine existing conditions in the firm (Chapter 18).

MBO TEAM:

A group of MBO specialists and consultants within a particular company (Chapter 17).

MC:

See MBO consultant.

MEASUREMENT METHOD:

The way in which the degree of attainment of an objective is to be determined (Chapter 10).

MOM:

See Managerial Objectives Meeting.

MOS:

See Managerial Objectives Seminar.

MS:

See MBO Specialist.

NON-MEASURABLE AREA:

An unsuitable effectiveness area as the associated objective is not measurable (Chapter 6).

O:

See Objectives.

OBJECTIVE RECORD SHEET (ORS):

A form used to record a single objective of one effectiveness area and the priority, measurement method, and associated activities of that objective (Chapter 11).

OBJECTIVES (O):

Effectiveness standards which are as specific, as time-bounded, and as measurable as possible (Chapter 3).

ORGANISATION:
All the factors which influence behaviour within a social system that are common to essentially unrelated positions (Chapter 12).

ORS:
See Objective Record Sheet.

OUTPUTS:
What a manager achieves, or is to achieve, rather than what he does (Chapter 6).

OVERLAP:
When two positions are responsible for the same thing. May refer to effectiveness areas or objectives (Chapter 7).

OVERLOAD:
Levels of objectives set too high to be attainable. (Chapter 8).

PERSONAL EFFECTIVENESS:
The extent to which a manager achieves his own private objectives (Chapter 1).

PLAN, A:
A sequence of activities (Chapter 9).

PREDICTIVE OBJECTIVE:
An objective based on a prediction rather than a plan (Chapter 8).

PRIORITY:
The relative importance of an objective indicated by the number 1, 2 or 3 (Chapter 8).

PROJECT EFFECTIVENESS AREA:
A common effectiveness area concerned with a manager's special projects (Chapter 4).

RATCHET PRINCIPLE:
Setting a slightly higher objective than the one previously attained (Chapter 8).

ROLL-DOWN:

Passing objectives downward (Chapter 16).

ROLL-UP:

Passing objectives upward (Chapter 16).

SCHEDULE:

A plan with timings (Chapter 9).

SECOND-GENERATION START-UP:

A second attempt at MBO implementation (Chapter 18).

SPECIFIC EFFECTIVENESS AREAS:

Effectiveness areas specific to particular managerial positions rather than common to all (Chapter 5).

START-UP:

The process between the time a company first thinks seriously about MBO and the time it commits major resources to implementing it (Chapter 18).

STRETCH:

The difference between past and planned performance (Chapter 8).

SUBORDINATE:

A person over whom a manager has authority and for whose work he is responsible (Chapter 12).

SUBORDINATE EFFECTIVENESS AREA:

A common effectiveness area concerned with the effectiveness of a manager's subordinate (Chapter 4).

SUPERIOR:

A person having authority over a manager and who is responsible for the manager's work (Chapter 12).

SYSTEMS EFFECTIVENESS AREA:

A common effectiveness area concerned with a manager's maintenance of budget, procedural and administrative control systems (Chapter 4).

TEAM OBJECTIVES MEETING (TOM):
A three day meeting between a manager and all his subordinates at which unit and individual effectiveness areas are established and appropriate changes made in unit organisation structure, policies, and procedures (Chapter 14).

TIME AREA:
An item on which a manager spends a great deal of time but which is not an effectiveness area (Chapter 6).

TOM:
See Team Objectives Meeting.

UEA:
See Unit Effectiveness Areas.

UED:
See Unit Effectiveness Description.

UNDERLAP:
When no position has been assigned the responsibility for a result it is necessary to obtain. May refer to effectiveness areas or objectives (Chapter 7).

UNDERLOAD:
Levels of objectives set so low that they would be attained without effort (Chapter 8).

UNIT EFFECTIVENESS AREAS:
The full set of effectiveness areas for a managerial position and all subordinate positions but not necessarily including the common effectiveness areas (Chapter 5).

UNIT EFFECTIVENESS DESCRIPTION:
A written statement specifying the effectiveness areas, effectiveness standards and authority of a unit, its superior and its managers (Chapter 7).

VERTICAL ALIGNMENT:
When the manager's effectiveness areas and objectives mesh well with those of other managers above and below him (Chapter 7).

WORRY AREA:
An effectiveness area a manager shows as his own because he does not expect another manager whose area it is, to deal with it effectively without intervention (Chapter 6).

Appendix B
Bibliography

Guide to Bibliography

As this bibliography of 170 items on MBO and related topics is extensive, this guide is provided for those with particular interests concerning:

BOOKS ABOUT MBO:

7, 12, 16, 27, 29, 45, 53, 55, 56, 60, 64, 82, 86, 92, 105, 109, 110, 112, 118, 126, 136, 141, 150, 163

BOOKS OF REFERENCE ABOUT MBO:

10, 33, 49, 97, 98, 99, 100, 101, 132

BOOKS ON TOPICS ASSOCIATED WITH MBO:

3, 8, 9, 13, 23, 26, 30, 31, 36, 67, 75, 83, 84, 88, 103, 106, 108, 115, 117, 119, 124, 133, 142, 143, 145, 148, 149, 154, 166

CORPORATE OBJECTIVES REFERENCES:

2, 3, 14, 15, 32, 34, 48, 52, 61, 63, 64, 68, 91, 117, 122, 137, 142, 145, 148, 149, 154, 155, 166

ADMINISTRATIVE REFERENCES:

1, 5, 17, 20, 21, 35, 39, 41, 79, 115, 116, 135, 152

PERFORMANCE REVIEW REFERENCES:

54, 87, 88, 89, 96, 103, 104, 125, 128, 130, 139, 169

MBO EVALUATIVE REFERENCES:

5, 43, 44, 52, 120, 158, 159, 160, 168

SPECIAL APPLICATIONS REFERENCES:

18, 19, 45, 74, 80, 98, 99, 100, 101, 116, 134, 165

GENERAL MBO ARTICLES:

6, 22, 25, 37, 40, 42, 57, 58, 59, 62, 65, 68, 72, 81, 82, 93, 94, 95, 107, 113, 114, 140, 146, 147, 151, 153, 162, 167, 170

HUMAN SIDE REFERENCES:

4, 44, 46, 47, 50, 66, 71, 73, 76, 77, 78, 84, 85, 88, 90, 96, 111, 123, 127, 131, 161, 169

TIME MANAGEMENT REFERENCES:

28, 69, 83, 129

PLANNING INFORMATION AND CONTROL REFERENCES:

11, 24, 51, 63, 64, 67, 70, 75, 102, 121, 133, 138, 144, 154, 156, 157, 165

KEY U.S.A. REFERENCES:

7, 27, 29, 53, 86, 88, 105, 109, 141, 149, 163

KEY U.K. REFERENCES:

16, 38, 55, 56, 59, 60, 120

KEY CANADIAN REFERENCES:

5, 17, 20, 21, 64, 164

1   Air Force Logistics Command, *Results-Oriented Management; Management by (Job) Objectives*, AFLC Pamphlet 25-2, 7th Nov. 1962.

2   Ansoff, H. Igor, 'Company Objectives: Blueprint or Blue Sky?', *Management Review*, Sept. 1962, pp. 85–90.

3   ———, *Corporate Strategy*, McGraw-Hill Book Co., New York, 1965.

4   Argyris, C., 'T-Groups for Organisational Effectiveness', *Harvard Business Review*, Mar.–Apr. 1964, pp. 60–74.

5   Baker, Walter, *Management by Objectives: A Philosophy and Style of Management for the Public Sector*, Canadian Public Administration, Autumn, 1969.

6   Barry, Anthony, 'Developing Tomorrow's Managers', *Personnel Magazine*, Jan. 1966, pp. 16–19, 23.

7   Batten, J. D., *Beyond Management by Objectives*, American Management Association, New York, 1966.

8   Batten, J. D., *Developing a Tough Minded Climate for Results*, AMA, New York, 1963.

9   ——, *Tough Minded Management*, AMA, New York, 1963.

10   Bennett, C. L., 'Defining the Manager's Job', *Manual of Position Descriptions*, AMA, New York, 1958.

11   Bishop, S. V., *Business planning and control*, Institute of Chartered Accountants in England and Wales, General Educational Trust, June 1966.

12   Bittel, Lester R., *Management By Exception: Systematizing and Simplifying the Managerial Job*, McGraw-Hill Book Co., New York, 1964.

13   Bower, Marvin, *The Will to Manage*, McGraw-Hill Book Co., New York.

14   Boyd, Harper W. Jr. and Levy, Sidney J., 'What Kind of Corporate Objectives', *Journal of Marketing*, Vol. 30, Oct. 1966, pp. 53–85.

15   Branch, M. C., *The Corporation Planning Process*, AMA, New York, 1962.

16   British-Pathe: Management by Objectives (film with John W. Humble), British-Pathe, London, 1969, 27 minute, colour 16 mm.

17   Burser, F. W., *Management by Objectives*, Management Services, Ottawa, Sept. 1969.

18   *Business Management*, 'MBO in R & D', Feb. 1970, pp. 28–31.

19   Carey, L. A., 'Setting Long-Range Sales Objectives in a Large Corporation', *Budgeting*, Mar. 1965, pp. 11–12.

20   Carson, John, J., *The Changing Scope of the Public Servant*, Canadian Public Administration, Winter 1968, pp. 407–13.

21   Chartrand, P. J., 'Manpower Planning', *Business Quarterly*, Spring 1969, pp. 65–73.

22   Conference Board Record, 'Setting Targets for the Staff', Oct. 1964, pp. 32–34.

23   Cordiner, R. J., *New Frontiers For Professional Managers*, McGraw-Hill Book Co., New York, 1956.

24 Dearden, John, 'Can Management Information Be Automated?', *Harvard Business Review*, Mar.–Apr. 1964.

25 Doris, Edward, H., 'Management by Objectives', *Budgeting*, May 1966, pp. 13–18.

26 Drucker, Peter F., *Concept of the Corporation*, The John Day Company, Inc., New York, 1946.

27 ——, *The Effective Executive*, Harper & Row, New York, 1966.

28 ——, 'How Effective Executives Use Their Time', *Management Review*, Mar. 1968, pp. 18–22.

29 ——, *Managing for results*, Heinemann, London, Harper & Row, New York, 1964.

30 ——, *The New Society: The Anatomy of the Industrial Order*, Harper & Row, New York, 1950.

31 ——, *The Practice of Management*, Harper & Brothers, New York, 1954.

32 *Dun's Review*, 'Rocky Road to Company Goals', Vol. 92, Sept. 1968, pp. 45–50.

33 Enell, J. W. and Haas, George H., *Setting Standards for Executive Performance*, (Research Study No. 42), AMA, New York, 1960.

34 Ewing, David, *Long-range planning for management*, revised edition, Harper & Row, New York, and London, 1963.

35 Finer, Herman, 'Administrative Responsibility in Democratic Government', *Public Administration Review*, Summer 1941, pp. 336–505.

36 Folsom, M. B., *Executive Decision Making*, McGraw-Hill Book Co., New York, 1962.

37 Ford, Charles H., 'If You're Problem-Oriented, You're In Trouble', *Business Management*, Vol. 35, Feb. 1969, pp. 24–28.

38 Forrest, Andrew, *The Manager's Guide to Setting Targets*, The Industrial Society London, 1966.

39 Friedrich, C. J., 'Public Policy and the Nature of Administrative Responsibility, in C. J. Friedrich and E. S. Mason (eds.), *Public Policy*, Harvard University Press, Cambridge, 1940, pp. 3–24.

40   Frost, Andrew, 'Towards more effective management by setting targets', *Industrial Welfare*, Oct. 1965, pp. 250–51.

41   Garrett, John and Walker, S. D., *Management by Objectives in the Civil Service*, HMSO, CAS Occasional Papers 10, 1969.

42   Glasner, Daniel M., 'Patterns of Management by Results', *Business Horizons*, Vol. 12, Feb. 1969, pp. 37–40.

43   Granger, Charles H., 'The Hierarchy of Objectives', *Harvard Business Review*, Vol. 42, May–June 1964.

44   Gross, Bertram M., 'What are Your Organisation's Objectives?', *Human Relations*, London, Vol. 18, No. 3, pp. 195–216.

45   Guest, R. H., *Organisational Change: The Effect of Successful Leadership*, Dorsey Press, Homewood, Ill., 1962.

46   Guth, William D. and Tagiuri, Renato, 'Personal Values and Corporate Strategies', *Harvard Business Review*, Vol. 43, No. 5, Sept.–Oct. 1965.

47   Herzberg, F., 'One More Time: How Do You Motivate Employees?', *Harvard Business Review*, Jan.–Feb. 1968.

48   Hewkin, J. W. and Kempner, T., *Is Corporate Planning Necessary?*, British Institute of Management Information Summary 138, London, 1968.

49   Higgenson, M. Valliant, *Management Policies*, AMA Research Study 75, New York, 1966.

50   Hoffer, E., *The True Believer*, Harper & Row, New York, 1951.

51   Holstein, Wm. K., 'Production Planning and Control Integrated', *Harvard Business Review*, May–June 1968.

52   Howell, Robert A., 'A Fresh Look at Management by Objectives', *Business Horizons*, Vol. 10, Autumn 1967, pp. 51–58.

53   Hughes, Charles L., *Goal Setting: Key to Individual and Organisational Effectiveness*, AMA, New York, 1965.

54   ——, 'Why Goal Oriented Performance Reviews Succeed and Fail', *Personnel Journal*, June 1966.

55   Humble, J. W., *Improving Business Results*, McGraw-Hill, U.K., 1968.

56   Humble, J. W., *Improving Management Performance*, Management Publications Ltd., London, 1969.

57   ——, *Management by Objectives*, Industrial Education and Research Foundation, London, 1967.

58   ——, 'Management by Objectives', International Review Conference, 9th Dec. 1969.

59   ——, 'Management by Objectives', *Directors' Guide to Management Techniques*, Chapter 2.

60   ——, Management by Objectives Study Material for the 16 mm film, British-Pathé, London, 1969.

61   Huston, Charles L., Jr., 'Setting Corporate Objectives', *Dun's Review and Modern Industry*, Oct. 1962, pp. 62–63.

62   IMI and Irish National Productivity Committee, *Planning your business*, Dublin Stationery Office for National Industrial Economic Council, 1966.

63   *Iron Age*, 'Managing by Objectives – Why It's Tough', Vol. 204, 29th Sept. 1969, pp. 98–100.

64   Irwin, Patrick, *Business Planning: Key to Profit Growth*, Ryerson Press, Toronto, 1969.

65   Ivancevich, J. M., 'The Theory and Practice of Management by Objectives', *Michigan Business Review*, Vol. 21, Mar. 1969, pp. 13–16.

66   Jaques, E., *The Changing Culture of a Factory*, Tavistock Publications, 1951.

67   Jerome, W. T., *Executive Control – The Catalyst*, Wiley, New York, 1961.

68   ——, *Towards a Philosophy of Management*, Financial Executive, Aug. 1965, pp. 19–22.

69   Jones, Curtis H., 'The Money Value of Time', *Harvard Business Review*, July, Aug. 1968.

70   Juran, J. M., 'Universals in Management Planning and Controlling', *The Management Review*, Nov. 1954.

71   Kehoe, P. T. and Reddin, W. J., *Organization Health Survey*, Organizational Tests Ltd., N.B., 1970.

72   Knight, M. W. B. and Humble, J. W., 'Management by Objectives', *Statist*, 8th Apr. 1966, pp. 872–879.

73 Korman, A. K., 'Consideration, Initiating Structure and Organizational Criteria – A review', *Personnel Psychology*, Vol. 19, Winter 1966, pp. 349–361.

74 Leathers, James O., 'Applying Management by Objectives to the Sales Force', *Personnel*, Sept.–Oct. 1967, pp. 45–50.

75 LeBreton, Preston, Henning, Dale A., *Planning Theory*, Prentice-Hall, N.J., 1961.

76 Likert, Rensis, *The Human Organization*, McGraw-Hill Book Co., New York, 1967.

77 ——, 'Measuring Organizational Performance', *Harvard Business Review*, Vol. 36, No. 2, Mar.–Apr. 1968.

78 ——, *New Patterns of Management*, McGraw-Hill Book Co., New York, 1961.

79 Lindblom, Charles E., 'The Science of Muddling Through', *Public Administration Review*, Vol. 19, 1959–1964.

80 Locker, L., *Introducing Management by Objectives into the South Western Electricity Board*, South Western Electricity Board, London, 1969.

81 Mahler, Walter R., 'A "Systems" Approach to Managing by Objectives', *Systems and Procedures Journal*.

82 Marvin, Phillip, *Management Goals: Guidelines and Accountability*, Dow Jones-Irwin, Homewood, Ill., 1968.

83 McCay, James T., *The Management of Time*, Prentice-Hall, Englewood Cliffs, N.J., 1959.

84 McClelland, D. C., *The Achieving Society*, D. Van Nostrand Company, Inc. Princeton, N.J., 1961.

85 ——, 'Business Drive and National Achievement', *Harvard Business Review*, July–Aug. 1962, pp. 99–112.

86 McConkey, D. D., *How to Manage by Results*, AMA, New York, 1965.

87 ——, 'Results Approach to Evaluating Managerial Performance', *Advanced Mangement Journal*, Vol. 32, Oct. 1967, pp. 18–26.

88 McGregor, D. V., *The Human Side of Enterprise*, McGraw-Hill Book Co., New York, 1960.

89   McGregor, Douglas, 'An Uneasy Look at Performance Appraisal, *Harvard Business Review*, May–June 1957, pp. 89–95.

90   McNair, M. P., 'What Price Human Relations', *Harvard Business Review*, Mar.–Apr. 1957, pp. 15–39.

91   Mee, John F., 'Objectives in a Management Philosophy', *Business Horizons*, Dec. 1956.

92   Mendleson, J. L., *Managerial Goal Setting: An Exploration into Meaning and Measurement*, Unpublished dissertation, Michigan State University, 1968.

93   ——, 'Personal Targets For Effective Management', *Canadian Business*, Jan. 1970.

94   Meredith, James E. Jr., 'Management by Objectives', *The Office*, Vol. 69, Jan. 1969.

95   Metropolitan Life Ins. Co., *Management by Objectives*, Management Services Dept., New York, 1965.

96   Meyer, Herbert H., Kay, Emanuel and French, John R. P. Jr., 'Split Roles in Performance Appraisal', *Harvard Business Review*, XLIII, Jan.—Feb. 1965, pp. 123–129.

97   Miller, Ernest C., *Objectives and standards approach to planning and control*, AMA, New York, AMA Research Study 74, 1966.

98   ——, *Objectives and Standards of Performance in Financial Management*, AMA, New York, 1968.

99   ——, *Objectives and Standards of Performance in General Management*, AMA, New York, 1967.

100 ——, *Objectives and Standards of Performance in Marketing Management*, AMA, New York, 1967.

101 ——, *Objectives and Standards of Performance in Production Management*, AMA, New York, 1967.

102 Miller, Robert W., 'How To Plan And Control With PERT', *Harvard Business Review*, Mar.–Apr. 1962.

103 Miner, John B., *The Management of Ineffective Performance*, McGraw-Hill Book Co.

104 NCIB, 'Management by Objectives or Appraisal by Results', The Conference Board Record, NCIB, New York, Vol. 3, No. 7, July 1966.

105 NCIB, *Managing By And With Objectives*, Studies in Personnel Policy No. 212, New York, 1968.

106 Newman, W., Summer, C. E. and Warren, E. K., *The Process of Management*, 2nd edition, Prentice-Hall, Englewood Cliffs, N.J., Ch. 18, 1967.

107 Norman, D. M., 'You Can Improve Management Effectiveness', *Canadian Business*, June 1969, pp. 64–70.

108 Odiorne, G. S., *How Managers Make Things Happen*, Prentice-Hall, Englewood Cliffs, N.J., 1961.

109 ——, *Management by objectives: a system of managerial leadership*, Pitman, New York, 1965.

110 ——, *Management Decisions By Objectives*, Prentice-Hall, Inc., Englewood Cliffs, N.J., 1969.

111 ——, 'The Trouble with Sensitivity Training', *ASTD Journal*, Oct. 1963.

112 Olsson, David E., *Management by Objectives*, Pacific Books, Palo Alto, Calif., 1968.

113 Owen, D. E. P., B.Sc., 'Management Techniques; Setting Objectives', *The Chartered Mechanical Engineer*, Sept. 1966, pp. 388–392.

114 Panton, F. S., 'Management by objectives', *Management in Nigeria*, May–June 1967, pp. 23–26.

115 Parkinson, C. N., *Parkinson's Law*, John Murray, London, 1958.

116 Pascoe, B. J., 'Case History of Management by Objectives Within The Civil Service', Royal Naval Supply and Transport Service Ministry of Defence (Navy), London, 1969.

117 Payne, Bruce, *Planning for company growth: the executive's guide to effective long range planning*, McGraw-Hill Book Co., New York, 1963.

118 Pelissier, Raymond, Review of *Improving Business Results*, by John Humble, *Personnel Administration*, May–June 1970.

119 *Political and Economic Planning, Thrusters and Sleepers*, Allen & Unwin, London, 1965.

120   Raia, Anthony P., 'Goal Setting and Self Control', *Journal of Management Studies*, Vol. 1–2, Feb. 1965, pp. 34–53.

121   ——, 'A Second Look at Goals and Controls', *California Management Review*, Vol. 55, Summer 1966, pp. 65–69.

122   Reddin, W. J., *Corporate Objectives Conference Course Material*, Management By Objectives Ltd., Fredericton, N.B., 1970.

123   ——, *Job Enrichment Form*, Organizational Tests Ltd., Fredericton, N.B., 1970.

124   ——, *Managerial Effectiveness*, McGraw-Hill Book Co., New York and U.K., 1970.

125   ——, *Managerial Objectives Conference Part One Course Material*, Management By Objectives Ltd., Fredericton, N.B., 1970.

126   ——, *Managerial Objectives Seminar Course Material*, Management By Objectives Ltd., Fredericton, N.B., 1970.

127   ——, *Team Objectives Meeting Course Material*, Management By Objectives Ltd., Fredericton, N.B., 1970.

128   ——, and O'Brien, D., *Time Usage Diary*, Organizational Tests Ltd., Fredericton, N.B., 1970.

129   ——, and Sullivan, B., *Managerial Effectiveness Biography*, Organizational Tests Ltd., Fredericton, N.B., 1970.

130   Rowe, Kay H., 'An Appraisal of Appraisals', *Journal of Management Studies*, Vol. 1, No. 1, Mar. 1964, pp. 1–25.

131   Rowell, K., *Employee Survey*, Organizational Tests Ltd., Fredericton, N.B., 1970.

132   Rowland, Virgil K., *Managerial Performance Standards*, AMA, New York, 1960, pp. 35–36.

133   St Thomas, Charles E., *Practical business planning; a manager's guide*, AMA, New York, 1965.

134   Sanders, George S., 'The Management of Research', *Chemistry and Industry*, 1965, pp. 2076–2079.

135   Scanlan, Burt K., 'Quantifying the Qualifiable, or Can Results Management Be Applied to the Staff Man's Job?' *Personnel Journal*, Vol. 47, Mar. 1968, pp. 162–6; 203.

136   ——, *Results Management in Action*, Management Centre of Cambridge, Cambridge, Mass., 1967.

137   Schaffer, R. H., *Managing by Total Objectives*, AMA, New York, 1964.

138   ——, 'Putting Action Into Planning', *Harvard Business Review*, Nov.–Dec. 1967.

139   Scheid, Phil N., 'Charter Of Accountability for Executives', *Harvard Business Review*, July–Aug. 1965.

140   Schleh, Edward C., 'Management by Objective: Some Principles for Making it Work', *The Management Review*, Nov. 1959, pp. 26–33.

141   ——, *Management by results: the dynamics of profitable management*, McGraw-Hill Book Co., New York, 1961.

142   Scott, Brian W., *Long-range planning in American Industry*, AMA, New York, 1965.

143   Simon, Herbert A., *Administrative Behaviour*, 2nd edition, Glencoe Free Press, N.Y., 1957.

144   Simpkins, John J., 'Planning for Management by Objectives', *Systems & Procedures Journal*, Jan.–Feb. 1966, pp. 32–37.

145   Sloan, Alfred P., *My years with General Motors*, Doubleday, New York, 1963.

146   Smith, Charles H., 'Management by Objectives as a Communication Device', in *Superior-Subordinate Communication in Management*, Research Study No. 52, AMA, New York, 1961.

147   *Steel Magazine*, 'Managing by Objectives', Vol. 160, Mar. 6, 1967, pp. 73, 5.

148   Steiner, G. A., *Managerial Long-Range Planning*, McGraw-Hill Book Co., New York, 1963.

149   ——, *Top Management Planning*, The MacMillan Company, New York, 1969.

150   Stewart, Nathaniel, *Strategies of Managing for Results*, Prentice-Hall, Englewood Cliffs, N.J., 1966.

151 Stull, R. A., 'Determining Management Objectives', *Rydges*, Apr. 1963.

152 Stumpf, Charles F., 'Administration by Objectives', *Hospital Administration*, Winter 1961, pp. 43–50.

153 Thompson, James, *Organizations in Action*, McGraw-Hill Book Co., New York, 1967, Ch. 3.

154 Thompson, S., *How companies plan*, AMA, New York, 1962.

155 Tilles, Seymour, 'How to Evaluate Corporate Strategy', *Harvard Business Review*, Vol. 41, No. 4, July–Aug. 1963.

156 ——, 'The Manager's Job: A Systems Approach', *Harvard Business Review*, Jan. 1963.

157 Toedt, Theodore A., 'Meaning of Control,' *Hospitals*, 16th Dec. 1958.

158 Tosi, H. L. and Carroll, S. J., 'Managerial reaction to Management by Objectives', *Academy of Management Journal*, Vol. No. 4, Dec. 1968, pp. 415–426.

159 ——, 'Some factors affecting the success of "management by objectives",' *Journal of Management Studies*, Vol. 7, No. 2, May 1970, pp. 209–223.

160 ——, Henry L. Jr. and Carroll, Stephen J., 'Some Structural Factors Related to Goal Influence in the Management by Objectives Process', *MSU Business Topics*, Vol. 17, Spring 1969, pp. 45–50.

161 Trickett, J. M., 'Fulfilling Individual Needs in Management Development', *Personnel*, May 1957.

162 Valentine, R. F., 'Laying the Groundwork for Goal Setting', *Personnel*, Vol. 43, Jan.–Feb. 1966, pp. 34–41.

163 ——, *Performance Objectives for Managers*, AMA, New York, 1966.

164 Villeneuve, Jacques P., 'Effective Development and Utilization of Management Talent', MSS unpublished.

165 Villers, R., *Research and Development: Planning and Control*, Financial Executives Research Foundation, New York, 1964.

166 Warren, E. Kirby, *Long-range planning: the executive viewpoint*, Prentice-Hall, Inc. Englewood Cliffs, N.J., 1966.

167   Westinghouse Electric Corporation, *Management Performance Objectives*, Management Guide GM—7 (revised), Pittsburgh, Mar. 1963, p. 2.

168   Wickens, J. D., 'Management by Objectives: An Appraisal', *Journal of Management Studies*, Vol. 5, No. 3, Oct. 1968, pp. 365–379.

169   Wickstrom, Walter S., 'Management by Objectives or Appraisal by Results', *The Conference Board Record*, New York, Vol. 3, July 1966, pp. 27–31.

170   Wrapp, H. E., 'Good Managers Don't Make Policy Decisions', *Harvard Business Review*, Sept.–Oct. 1967.

Index